WALKING IN THE NEW FOREST

30 WALKS IN THE NEW FOREST
NATIONAL PARK

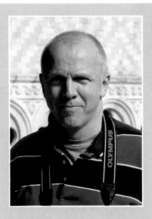

About the Author

Steve Davison is a freelance writer and photographer who has lived in Berkshire for over twenty years. He has written for a number of outdoor magazines and other publications, including local and national newspapers, specialising in hill walking and European travel, with interests in nature, geology and the countryside. A keen hill walker for many years and a Mountain Leader, Steve has also worked as a part-time outdoor education instructor. He is also a member of the Outdoor Writers and Photographers Guild. Find out more about him out at www.steve-davison.co.uk.

Other Cicerone guides by the author
The Great Stones Way
The Kennet and Avon Canal
The Ridgeway National Trail
Walking in the Chilterns
Walking in the North Wessex Downs
Walking in the Thames Valley

WALKING IN THE NEW FOREST

30 WALKS IN THE NEW FOREST NATIONAL PARK

by Steve Davison

JUNIPER HOUSE, MURLEY MOSS,
OXENHOLME ROAD, KENDAL, CUMBRIA LA9 7RL
www.cicerone.co.uk

© Steve Davison 2012
First edition 2012, reprinted 2016 and 2019 (with updates)
ISBN: 978 1 85284 637 4

Printed in China on behalf of Latitude Press Ltd.

A catalogue record for this book is available from the British Library.

All photographs are by the author unless otherwise stated.

© Crown copyright 2016.
OS PU100012932.

Updates to this Guide

While every effort is made by our authors to ensure the accuracy of guidebooks as they go to print, changes can occur during the lifetime of an edition. Any updates that we know of for this guide will be on the Cicerone website (www.cicerone.co.uk/637/updates), so please check before planning your trip. We also advise that you check information about such things as transport, accommodation and shops locally. Even rights of way can be altered over time. We are always grateful for information about any discrepancies between a guidebook and the facts on the ground, sent by email to updates@cicerone.co.uk or by post to Cicerone, Juniper House, Murley Moss, Oxenholme Road, Kendal LA9 7RL.

Register your book: To sign up to receive free updates, special offers and GPX files where available, register your book at www.cicerone.co.uk.

Front cover: Looking west along the Beaulieu River at Longwater Lawn (Walk 20)

CONTENTS

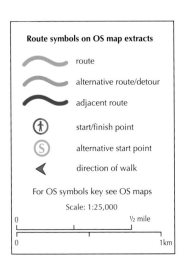

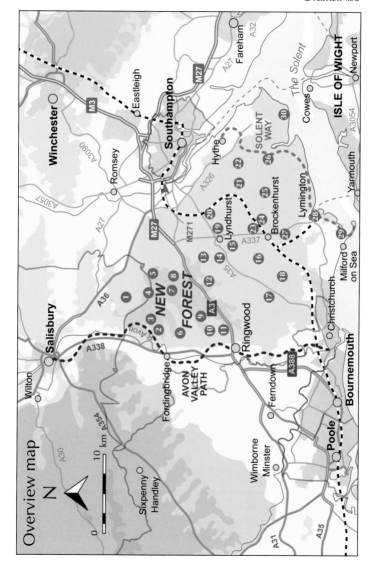

Overview map

N

Looking west from Cockley Hill towards Godshill Ridge (Walk 2)

INTRODUCTION

The New Forest, or the Nova Foresta as it was known in the Domesday Book, is a unique and captivating landscape of open heath and ancient woodland tucked into south-west Hampshire and south-east Wiltshire. 'Created' by William the Conqueror in 1079 as a royal hunting ground, the New Forest has, for the last 900 years, owed its very existence to the influence of man and his animals.

To many, a key feature of the New Forest's natural beauty is the ancient and ornamental woods, and here can

New Forest National Park sign near Rockford (Walk 10); these are placed where roads enter the New Forest National Park

be found the greatest concentration of 'veteran' trees in western Europe. However, there is much more on offer, including 42km (26 miles) of coastline, the largest area of lowland heath in Britain and three-quarters of the valley mires in north-west Europe, as well as picture-postcard thatched cottages, ancient churches and cosy pubs. And

An old tree in Queen Bower Wood (Walk 16)

all this located within Britain's smallest national park, covering just 570 square kilometres (220 square miles).

The New Forest may not be a very hilly landscape and there are no sweeping mountain views, but a walk in the Forest takes you into a part of Southern Britain that William the Conqueror would probably still recognise. Couple that with the fleeting glimpses of wildlife – a deer suddenly stops to look before magically disappearing in the blink of an eye, birdsong mingles with the rustle of the wind in the trees, wildflowers add splashes of colour to the beauty of the enchanting woods, the commoners' stock grazes the land as it has done for centuries – and you have all the ingredients that make walking in the New Forest National Park such a unique and rewarding experience.

However, this is not some woodland theme park; the Forest is a working environment. Around 7000 commoners' animals graze the open forest, one quarter of the park is farmland and the forests still produce many tonnes of timber per year. Remember, it is these very activities that have helped to preserve the New Forest over the centuries.

PLANTS AND WILDLIFE

The New Forest has a patchwork of habitats that have been shaped since prehistoric times by man and his animals. Each offers a rich variety of plants and animals, and for anyone wishing to identify the plants, fungi, animals and birds that they might see while out walking, it's worth carrying a guidebook, along with a pair of binoculars.

Trees

Although less than half of the national park is woodland, woods are a key feature of its natural beauty, with native trees ranging from the coniferous English Yew and Scots Pine to broad-leaved species such as the common oak, beech and silver birch.

A more exotic tree is the Wellingtonia, or giant sequoia, found along Rhinefield Drive (Walk 16). At a height of 55m, these may take the title of the tallest trees in the forest; however, it is the native oaks, such as the Knightwood Oak (Walk 14), that lay claim to being some of the biggest. These trees have been pollarded: when it was young the top of the tree was cut off, allowing new growth on multiple branches, resulting in tree trunks with a very large circumference but short height. Pollarding was a traditional way to harvest wood sustainably for fencing and firewood and the practice generally helps the tree to live longer – many examples in the Forest are between 400 and 600 years old.

Plants

Within the Forest there are around 2700 species of fungi and 700 species of wildflower, including rare species such as the blue marsh gentian (*Gentiana pneumonanthe*), yellow-green flowered bog orchid (*Hammarbya paludosa*) and the wild gladiolus (*Gladiolus illyricus*).

A much more common plant is gorse (*Ulex europaeus*), sometimes called 'furze', and its colourful yellow flowers can be seen throughout the open heath. Although the plant's spiky foliage should help to protect it from being eaten, it forms a vital part of the

11

(Clockwise from top left): cross-leaved heath, round-leaved sundew, gorse – known locally as furze – and colourful fly agaric

New Forest pony's diet, especially in winter, when other food is scarce.

Another widespread plant is common heather (*Calluna vulgaris*), also known as ling, which creates a colourful pale purple carpet across the open forest in late summer. Three other species of heather grow in the forest: bell heather (*Erica cinerea*), which thrives on acid heathland, blooms earlier in the summer with larger reddish-purple flowers; the pink-flowered cross-leaved heath (*Erica tetralix*), which prefers damper sites; and the much rarer Dorset heath (*Erica ciliaris*).

Common Cotton Grass (*Eriophorum angustifolium*), known locally as bog cotton, grows in the wetland areas, particularly valley mires. It is easily recognised by its characteristic white tufts which are most visible in late spring. Another plant which likes wet areas is the insectivorous round-leaved sundew (*Drosera rotundifolia*); the sticky scarlet hairs that cover the leaves are a perfect trap for small insects.

Two of the more common varieties of orchid are the common spotted orchid (*Dactylorhiza fuchsii*) and the heath spotted orchid (*Dactylorhiza maculata*). Both look very similar, with varying amounts of brown spots on their leaves and spikes of white to pink-purple flowers produced between June and August, although the common spotted orchid is the taller of the two species.

Reptiles

All six of Britain's native reptiles (snakes and lizards) are found in the New Forest, as well as three species of newt (smooth, palmate and great-crested), the common frog and common toad.

The six reptiles are:

- Adders (or viper) – Britain's only poisonous snake; light shade of grey or brown with a distinctive black zigzag marking along the length of the back
- Grass snake – dark green colour marked with black vertical bars and spots that run along the sides
- Smooth snake – greyish colour with usually two rows of darker brown or black markings along the back; also have round pupils to their eyes
- Slow worms – a type of legless lizard; have an almost cylindrical

Slow worm – one of Britain's six native reptiles that can be seen in the Forest

body with a polished-looking grey or brown colouration
- Common lizard – colouration can include shades of brown, grey and dark green
- Sand lizard – grey-beige colour with dark brown blotches; successfully reintroduced in 1998 having become extinct throughout Hampshire by about 1970

Birds

The Forest supports a wide range of birdlife, including many woodland birds such as woodpeckers, tawny owls, nuthatches and wood warblers. Areas of conifer are good for seeing siskin, along with the rare and diminutive firecrest. The Forest also supports a number of birds of prey, including sparrow hawks, buzzards, hobbies, kestrels and the rare honey buzzard.

Valley mires support important populations of snipe, curlew, lapwing and redshank, whereas the open heaths are home to the likes of woodlark and the UK's largest breeding population of the rare Dartford warbler, with summer visitors such as Montagu's harrier and the more nocturnal nightjar.

Along the riverbanks and estuaries you may see herons, little egrets or the vivid turquoise-blue and orange flash of a kingfisher darting along the river. The coastal stretches in winter see the arrival of large numbers of wildfowl and waders, including dark-bellied brent geese, wigeon and curlew.

Mammals

The Forest is home to a variety of animals, including large numbers of commoners' stock such as New Forest ponies and cows. There are five species of deer: fallow, roe, red, sika and muntjac, the most common being fallow and roe deer; the deer population is kept at around 3000 animals. Throughout the area, as with much of England, you will probably catch sight of the abundant grey squirrel which, sadly, has replaced the native red squirrel.

As dusk approaches you may be lucky and catch a glimpse of the elusive badger or the much rarer polecat, a new arrival to the Forest within the last few years. Other mammals that may be seen at dusk are bats; 13 of the 17 native species have been recorded in the New Forest, including the nationally rare Bechstein's and Barbastelle bats.

Invertebrates

There is a rich array of insects, including butterflies, moths, beetles and dragonflies. Many species are found in the ancient and ornamental woodlands, mainly due to the large quantities of dead wood found in these areas. One of the Forest's more striking beetles is the stag beetle. The males have large 'antlers' that they use for fighting with each other, hence the name. Butterflies include the silver-studded blue and dark green fritillary that live on the open heath, and silver-washed fritillary

Fallow deer at Bolderwood (Walk 12) – one of the five species of deer that can be seen in the Forest

and white admiral that can be found in wooded areas.

GEOLOGY

The New Forest is located in the Hampshire Basin – a shallow dip, or syncline, in the underlying chalk, surrounded by the chalk downs of Hampshire, Wiltshire and Dorset, along with the prominent chalk ridge on the Isle of Wight to the south, which includes The Needles. This chalk was laid down while the area was submerged by seas between 99 and 65 million years ago, in a period known as the Upper Cretaceous.

Subsequent seas, lakes and rivers in the Eocene period (from about 56 to 34 million years ago) laid down layers of gravel, sand and clay over the chalk. These layers have been tilted so that the oldest layers are to the north and more recent to the south, forming a slightly elevated plateau that slopes towards the coast. Rivers and streams have cut through this plateau to form gentle valleys between low flat-topped hills.

Overlying these layers, in large parts of the Forest, are superficial deposits of gravel that date from the Pleistocene period (2.5 million to 10,000 years ago) when Britain underwent periods of repeated glaciations. Although the ice sheets never reached as far south as the New Forest, the glacial rivers washed large quantities of flint gravel down from the chalk outcrops to the north. The final main geological event took place around 9000 years ago when the area that now forms the New Forest became separated from the Isle of Wight due to rising sea levels.

HISTORY OF THE NEW FOREST

The New Forest, recorded in the Domesday Book as Nova Foresta, was 'created' by William the Conqueror in 1079 as a royal hunting ground. At that time, the word 'forest' meant an area of countryside, not necessarily woodland, set aside for royal hunting. However, the area's history stretches back to at least the Bronze Age and at one time was known as Ytene, 'the place of the Jutes'. People who lived within the forest perambulation (or boundary) became subject to harsh Forest Law, although these laws were slightly relaxed in 1217 with the 'Charter of the Forest'. The Verderers were authorised by the Crown to deal with the day-to-day administration of the Forest.

Move forward a few hundred years to 1483 and the New Forest Act was passed allowing inclosures to be created, and the growing of timber became more important than protecting the deer. In the mid-1500s Henry VIII built large fortifications along the south coast, including ones at Hurst and Calshot. The last king to use his right to hunt in the Forest was James II in the 1680s. In the 17th and 18th centuries, the Verderers' powers were increased to help guard against offences undermining the planting and preservation of oak for ship-building; it took between 2500 and 3000 mature oak trees to make one Battle of Trafalgar ship, such as HMS *Victory*.

Because of the shift in emphasis to oak, deer (which along with other mammals can damage trees) became undesirable, and in 1851 the Deer Removal Act initiated the culling of virtually all of the deer in the Forest; luckily, some survived.

In 1877 the restrictions on common grazing were removed and the Verderers' Court was reformed through an Act of Parliament to become the guardians of commoners, common rights, and the Forest landscape. In 1924 the Forestry Commission took over the management of the New Forest.

During both World Wars the Forest played its part. Large areas were planted with conifer to provide a fast-growing source of timber, while some areas of open heath were ploughed and planted to provide crops. During WWII the Forest was home to several airfields, including Beaulieu Heath, Holmsley and Stoney Cross, along with the Ashley Walk Bombing Range (Walk 4), while the area around Lepe (Walk 30) played an important role in the D-Day campaign. Reminders of this time can also be seen at the Canadian Memorial (Walk 12), the Portuguese Fireplace (Walk 14) and St Nicholas' Church (Walk 24).

The grassy path through Roe Inclosure near the remains of Castle Piece, an old Iron Age fort (Walk 11)

The latest chapter in the New Forest's history began in 2005 when it gained National Park status, becoming the 14th national park in the UK, and the newly created park authority was given the task of helping to conserve this unique landscape for future generations.

17

WALKING IN THE NEW FOREST

The walks in this guide range from 5.2 to 16.3km (3¼ to 10 miles) and cover fairly level terrain, with only short climbs, making them suitable for all the family. Many of the routes follow well-defined tracks and paths, though some follow narrow and at times indistinct paths over the open heath and less-defined rides through forested areas where careful navigation may be required. On some of the routes you may have to step or jump across shallow streams and these will normally cause few problems. However, after heavy rainfall, streams can easily flood; if a stream or river is flooded the best option is to abandon the walk.

Make every effort to avoid disturbing the wildlife and keep dogs under close control, in particular between March and July when the Forest is home to ground-nesting birds such as the curlew and snipe.

As for the weather, summers in the New Forest tend to be fairly dry; this is also the time of year with the

Horse and foal at Woodgreen Common (Walk 3)

highest number of visitors, giving rise to traffic congestion is some areas. Spring and autumn offer some of the best walking conditions. Spring heralds new life in the Forest, with vivid greens on the trees, colourful displays of flowers and abundant birdsong. Late summer sees the heather on the open heath turn to a carpet of purple, and cool autumn nights herald a dramatic change, with the trees becoming clothed in spectacular shades of russet, gold and brown.

During the winter months, spells of rain can make some parts of the Forest very wet underfoot, and water levels can rise, making the crossing of some streams difficult, especially if walking with children. However, walking on a clear, frosty winter's day can be a magical experience.

Always choose clothing suitable for the season, along with a waterproof jacket, comfortable and waterproof footwear and a comfortable rucksack. On wet days gaiters or waterproof trousers can also be very useful. It's also worth carrying a basic first aid kit to deal with minor incidents.

Unfortunately, the New Forest is one area where you may come across ticks, especially in late spring and early summer. These small parasites are found in vegetation waiting to attach themselves to a passing host, whether that's an animal or walker.

You can reduce the risk of tick bites by:

- Wearing trousers and long-sleeved tops
- Tucking trousers into your socks, or wearing gaiters
- Staying on paths and trying to avoid walking through areas of long grass

If you do find a tick on you, either remove it by gripping it as close to the skin as possible with fine tweezers, and pulling steadily away from the skin in a single, smooth action, making sure not to squeeze the body of the tick; or use a specialised tick removal tool (follow the manufacturer's guidance). Some ticks carry the bacteria that can cause Lyme disease and this can be transmitted through a bite. The early signs of infection are prolonged flu-like symptoms often accompanied by an expanding circular rash – seek medical advice if you have been bitten and develop any such symptoms.

USING THE GUIDE

The route descriptions in this guidebook all follow the same format. The information box gives the start and finish location with the grid reference and parking details; the walk distance (km/miles); the time it will take to complete the walk; details of relevant OS Explorer maps; and details of any pubs or cafés along the way.

A short introduction gives a brief summary of the route, identifying any major points of interest, including villages. The walk is then described, accompanied by grid references to allow you to identify your location on the route map more easily.

Throughout the text you will find key landmarks highlighted in bold type; there is also additional information given for the places of interest passed on the route.

Times and distances

The distances quoted in the text have been measured from OS Explorer maps; note that the heights quoted on the maps are in metres and the grid lines are spaced at intervals of 1km. Distances are given in metric first, with approximate imperial conversions rounded to the nearest ¼, ½, ¾ or whole number. Estimated walking times are based on a walking speed of 4km per hour (2½ miles per hour), plus 10 minutes per 100m (300ft) of ascent. This should be treated as the minimum amount of walking time required to undertake the route and does not include any time for rests, lunch, photography, consulting the map or guidebook, or simply admiring the view – all of which can add substantially to the day's activity. Always pace the walk to the slowest member in the group, so that everyone can enjoy the walk.

MAPS

This guide contains extracts from the Ordnance Survey 1:25,000 Explorer series maps, with the route marked on, along with any shortcuts and extensions. These maps have a scale of 4cm to 1km (2½ inches to 1 mile) and offer a high level of detail, such as the location of a path in relation to a forest ride or

boundary, making route finding much easier. All of the walks can be found on the Ordnance Survey Explorer Map OL22 – New Forest, except for Walk 1 which also requires Map 131 – Romsey, Andover & Test Valley.

The grid references given in the guide are generated from the National Grid, and each map is divided by a series of vertical and horizontal lines to create a grid with a spacing of 1km. You can locate a point on a map, accurate to within 100m, using a grid reference made up of two letters and six numbers. The two letters correspond to the 100,000m square in which the grid reference lies. The first two digits of the six-figure number correspond to the vertical line ('easting') to the left of the point of interest, using the horizontal numbers along the bottom and top of the map; the third digit is the tenths of the square (equivalent to 100m). Next take the fourth and fifth digits, and move up the map to locate the horizontal line ('northing') below the point of interest; the last digit is again the number of tenths moving up through the square. Always remember: the horizontal numbers come before the vertical ones.

GETTING TO THE NEW FOREST

There are several ways of getting to the New Forest:

Road

The M27 from Southampton, accessible from the M3, reaches the north-east edge of the Forest to become the A31. The A31 also gives access from the south-west via Ringwood.

Rail
The mainline railway from London Waterloo to Weymouth passes through the Forest, with stations at Ashurst, Beaulieu Road, Brockenhurst and Sway and a branch line from Brockenhurst to Lymington. For information call National Rail Enquiries on 08457 484 950 (www.nationalrail.co.uk).

Coach
There are coach links from various UK locations to Lyndhurst, Brockenhurst and Lymington (National Express: 08717 818 178; www.nationalexpress.com).

Air
There are two airports that are convenient for the New Forest: Bournemouth Airport (www.bournemouthairport.com) to the west of the New Forest, is located about 9.7km (6 miles) from Bournemouth Central Station, and Southampton Airport (www.southamptonairport.com) to the north-east is adjacent to Southampton Parkway Station. Both stations have rail connections into the Forest.

Ferry
Brittany Ferries (www.brittany-ferries.co.uk) from France and Spain to Portsmouth, and France to Poole; Condor Ferries (www.condorferries.co.uk) from France and the Channel Islands to Weymouth, Poole and Portsmouth; Wightlink (www.wightlink.co.uk) operates ferries from Lymington and Portsmouth to the Isle of Wight; and Red Funnel (www.redfunnel.co.uk) operates between Southampton and the Isle of Wight.

One of the Isle of Wight ferries at Lymington. Ferries started sailing between the Isle of Wight and Lymington in 1830

GETTING AROUND THE NEW FOREST

The speed limit in all parts of the open forest is 40mph, reducing to 30mph in some areas. In open areas animals are free to roam across the road, and extra care is required, especially at night. Accidents with animals still do occur and around 100 are killed each year – all accidents with stock animals must be reported to the New Forest Verderers (see Appendix B). Some roads can be congested during the peak summer season, especially in and around Lyndhurst, and always remember to only park in designated car parks.

A few of the walks (Walks 20, 21, 23, 24 and 28) may be started from rail stations and some can be reached by using the local bus network. During the summer, the New Forest Tour bus operates in parts of the forest, giving access to some of the walks – you can hop on and off as many times as you like during the day. Always check for the latest information relating to trains and buses by using the contact details given in Appendix B. It's also worth getting copy of the handy New Forest Public Transport Guide and Map from local tourist offices, or online.

The New Forest has over 160km (100 miles) of waymarked cycle routes, much of it off-road and traffic free and there are several cycle hire centres; information on these is available from tourist information centres (Appendix B).

Looking west from the trig point near Whitefield Plantation on Ibsley Common (Walk 10)

FOOD AND DRINK

Some of the walks start at places where food and drink may be bought, whether it's a local shop, café or pub. Some offer opportunities for stopping off during the walk at a pub or shop, though these are not always conveniently placed round the route; brief details of places with pubs, shops and cafés are given in the information box at the start of each route, and where a route passes a particular pub or café, these are mentioned in the text. However, there is no guarantee that they'll be open when required. Therefore, it's always a good idea to carry some food and drink with you, along with a small 'emergency ration' in case of an unexpected delay.

WHERE TO STAY

The New Forest has a wide range of accommodation ranging from a

The Montagu Arms Hotel in Beaulieu (Walk 26)

youth hostel at Burley (0845 371 9309; www.yha.org.uk) through campsites and pubs with rooms to guest houses and hotels. For details visit the New Forest visitor website at www.thenewforest.co.uk. The Forestry Commission also has 10 camping and caravan sites ranging from Matley Wood (a small, basic site) to Holmsley with full facilities and 600 pitches (0845 130 8223; www.forestholidays.co.uk). Wild camping is not allowed within the New Forest.

COUNTRYSIDE CODES

While you are out enjoying these walks, please respect the countryside and follow both the Countryside Code and Forest Code.

Countryside Code
Be safe – plan ahead and follow any signs

Even when going out locally, it's best to get the latest information about where and when you can go; for example, your rights to go onto some areas of open land may be restricted while work is carried out, for safety reasons or during breeding seasons. Follow advice and local signs, and be prepared for the unexpected.

Leave gates and property as you find them

Please respect the working life of the countryside, as our actions can affect people's livelihoods, our heritage and

the safety and welfare of animals and ourselves.

Protect plants and animals, and take your litter home

We have a responsibility to protect our countryside now and for future generations, so make sure you don't harm animals, birds, plants or trees.

Keep dogs under close control

The countryside is a great place to exercise dogs, but it's every owner's duty to make sure their dog is not a danger or nuisance to farm animals, wildlife or other people.

Consider other people

Showing consideration and respect for other people makes the countryside a pleasant environment for everyone – at home, at work and at leisure.

Forest Code

1. Be safe and plan ahead – follow any signs and aim to be out of the Forest by dusk
2. Close all gates behind you unless they have been fastened open
3. Do not pick or remove plants or flowers
4. Do not feed or disturb the common stock – ponies, cattle and donkeys; give them space and do not touch them
5. Take your litter home and do not light fires
6. Keep to the existing tracks in the Forest when the birds nest on the

ground (1 March–31 July); at this time keep your dog close by you or you may be asked by a Forest Ranger or Keeper to put it on a lead

7. Keep below the Forest speed limit (40mph) and slow down when approaching walkers, riders or livestock

8. Do not park on the verges or in gateways; use one of the many car parks

9. Keep well away from any forestry work and obey the warning signs

ACCESS AND RIGHTS OF WAY

Large parts of the Forest are classed as open access land where you can freely roam. For this reason, rights of way are usually only marked outside the main open access areas. However, walking along tracks and paths is much easier, and during the nesting season (March to end of July) it is important to stay on existing routes so as not to disturb ground-nesting birds.

Rights of way are marked as follows:

- **Footpaths** Yellow Arrow – walkers only
- **Bridleways** Blue Arrow – walkers, cyclists and horse riders
- **Restricted byways** Purple Arrow – same as for a byway except no motorcycles or vehicles
- **Byways** Red Arrow – walkers, cyclists, horse riders, motorcycles and vehicles

THE NEW FOREST ONLINE

For up-to-date information on how to get there, public transport, accommodation and other visitor information, visit www.thenewforest.co.uk. For information about the national park, visit www.newforestnpa.gov.uk.

LONGER WALKS AND LONG-DISTANCE ROUTES

For anyone wanting a much longer walk, a quick look at the map will show that some of the walks could be easily combined (although directions for this are not given). The routes that can be easily combined are:

Shared (no extension required):
- Walks 2 (both versions) and 3
- Walks 4 (both versions) and 7 (both versions)
- Walks 7 (main route) and 9 (longer alternative)
- Walks 10 and 11
- Walks 15 and 16 (main route)
- Walks 24 and 27
- Walks 28 and 29

Short (less than 1km) extension required:
- Walks 2 (longer alternative) and 6
- Walks 4 (main route) and 6
- Walks 6 and 9 (longer alternative)
- Walks 12 and 13 (longer alternative)
- Walks 12 (longer alternative) and 14
- Walks 13 (longer alternative) and 14
- Walks 23 and 25 (longer alternative)
- Walks 24 and 25 (longer alternative)

Looking west along the Solent coastline near Lepe; on a very high tide this path can flood so you may have to use the road instead (Walk 30)

Long-distance routes

Finally, if you fancy a longer walk, two long-distance routes pass through parts of the New Forest; these are the Solent Way and the Avon Valley Path, both of which are visited by some of the walks in this guide.

The Solent Way is a 97km (60-mile) walking route from Milford on Sea in the west and Emsworth Harbour in the east. Following the path from west to east, it enters the national park at Hurst Spit near Keyhaven and passes through Lymington to Buckler's

Hard. From here it runs north along the Beaulieu River to pass Beaulieu and cross Beaulieu Heath before exiting the park at Hardley; about 30km of the Solent Way is within the park.

The 55km (34-mile) Avon Valley Path connects Christchurch in the south to Salisbury in the north. The path crosses the western boundary of the national park several times between Bisterne and North Charford, with about 11km of the path within the park.

WALK 1
Langley Wood and Hamptworth

Start/finish	Small roadside lay-by (SU 219 203) on the Redlynch to Hamptworth road beside the River Blackwater, or the Cuckoo Inn (SU 243 196)
Distance	8.5km (5¼ miles) or 8.9km (5½ miles)
Time	2½hrs or 2¾hrs
Maps	OS Explorer OL22 and 131
Refreshments	Cuckoo Inn, Hamptworth (01794 390302)

This fairly easy walk leads you through the peaceful woods on the northern edge of the New Forest National Park where it dips into Wiltshire. Along the way the walk passes through Langley Wood National Nature Reserve with its mix of broadleaved trees and varied wildlife, as well as visiting the little hamlet of Hamptworth with its picturesque, thatched Cuckoo Inn and duck pond. Unlike most of the national park, these woods are not open access, and the walk follows public rights of way throughout.

From the roadside lay-by, beside the bridge over the River Blackwater, cross over the road and go through a gap in the hedge to head south-west along a path signposted for Back Lane, following the hedge on the left. At the far end of the field cross a footbridge over the **River Blackwater** and keep ahead through the trees. ▶

Cross a stile and head along the enclosed path to cross another stile. Go between the houses and turn left along the lane, soon passing a picturesque, red-brick thatched cottage (Redwings). Continue down the lane, passing another thatched cottage (The Old Dairy), and keep along the track. Ignore the path off to the left, and at the track junction keep straight on to reach a split beside a byway sign. Continue straight on along the left fork, following the rhododendron-lined track; marked on the map, though not visible from the walk, is Hamptworth Lodge over to the left. Keep ahead along the main track to join a surfaced lane at **Home Farm** (SU 234 192).

The River Blackwater rises just east of Redlynch in Wiltshire and flows eastwards, mostly outside the national park, to join the River Test near Totton.

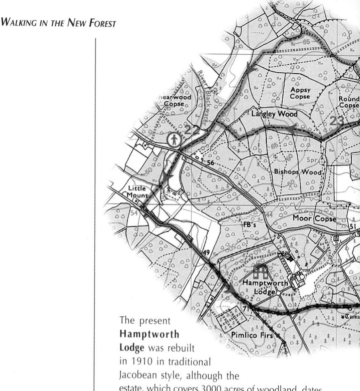

The present **Hamptworth Lodge** was rebuilt in 1910 in traditional Jacobean style, although the estate, which covers 3000 acres of woodland, dates back several centuries (limited public opening in the summer for guided tours; 01794 390700).

Continue straight on down the lane and just before the house on the left, turn left up the bank to follow a wide grassy path signposted to Elmtree Farm. Continue between the fence and hedge, later with trees to the right to reach a gate and path junction at the far side of the field. Do not go through the gate, but turn right down through the trees, ignoring a crossing tack to rejoin the lane. Turn left and at the junction beside the Wesleyan Chapel dated 1876 keep left (straight on), following Lyburn Road and soon passing **Manor Farm** to reach a T-junction (SU 244 196).

Have a look round the hamlet of **Hamptworth**. To the right is a small duck pond and thatched house

and to the left is a small green with footpath map and the very picturesque 18th-century thatched Cuckoo Inn – in the past this has been the village school and village shop. The footpath map was placed here by the

The pond and houses at Hamptworth

Redlynch Millennium Committee in association with
the parish council and Salisbury College to celebrate
the third millennium.

Cross over the road a few metres to the left and take
the path opposite, passing through the hedge to a kissing
gate and a footpath sign for Landford. Continue diagonally right across the field and just before the top right
corner turn right through a large gate and then left for
a few metres, to a signed path junction. Go left following the field edge on the left and turn right at the corner
heading downhill.

In the trees, cross a bridge over the River Blackwater
and continue up along the track for 500m, ignoring any
routes to the left and right. Go through the large gate,
keep ahead and follow the field edge on the right towards
North Common Farm. At the field corner with two gates,
turn right through the gate on the right into a field and
then left following the field edge on the left to cross a stile
in the corner. Turn left along the farm track, passing some
farm buildings, and continue straight on through the large
gate to follow a track down to a four-way track junction
(SU 243 206).

Go straight on along the gravel track with a golf
course on both sides. Ignore all crossing gravel paths
and continue along a path down through the trees. Cross
a stream via the footbridge and follow the narrow path
through the trees, passing a sign for Langley Woods
National Nature Reserve. Continue along the well-signed
path, with trees to the right and golf course to the left,
later following a sunken path gently uphill.

Although **Langley Woods National Nature Reserve**
now lies within the national park, it was originally
part of the Royal Forest of Melchet until the 16th
century. The reserve contains a mix of both pedun-
culate and sessile oak, along with small-leaved lime
and hazel. It is under minimum intervention management, where the felling and planting of trees is
avoided and dead wood is allowed to rot where it

falls. The woodland supports many plants and animals, from wood anemone, wood spurge and bluebells to silver-washed fritillary butterflies, common lizards and dormice, as well as deer and three species of woodpecker.

Woodland path through Langley Wood

Wood anemone (Anemone nemorosa) adds a splash of colour to the woods in early spring

These old medieval boundary banks were built to guide commoners' stock when they were being moved between the open commons.

Join a track and keep straight on to pass a kissing gate beside a large gate and continue along the lane. Where the lane bends left go right through a kissing gate to pass another sign for Langley Woods National Nature Reserve. Follow the track bounded by old earth banks to reach a marker post at a fork in the path (SU 232 206). ◄

Here there is a choice of routes: to continue on the main walk or take the alternative, slightly longer route.

To continue with the main walk fork left and head down through the trees, passing on your left an area dominated by alders (they prefer the wet soils here). Cross the footbridge and start climbing through an area of sweet chestnut trees and past a stand of Corsican pine. Keep straight on at the crossing path and follow the path as it bears to the right through an area of coppiced small-leaved lime and hazel. Turn left at the T-junction (the alternative route joins from the right), and shortly afterwards go through a kissing gate to the parking area.

Alternative route

At SU 232 206 take the right fork (straight on) and follow the circular walk signs in a semi-circle, before heading south to rejoin the main walk not far from the parking area.

WALK 2
Godshill and Castle Hill

Start/finish	Godshill Wood car park (SU 177 160), 1.3km (¾ mile) north from the B3078 at Godshill heading to Woodgreen, or Ashley Walk car park (SU 186 156)
Distance	7.6km (4¾ miles) or 11.6km (7¼ miles)
Time	2¼hrs or 3½hrs
Maps	OS Explorer OL22
Refreshments	The Fighting Cocks, Godshill (01425 652462)

From Godshill Wood car park the walk heads through Godshill Inclosure to reach Castle Hill, with a great view across the River Avon. Then it's along lanes, paths and tracks to reach Godshill and the Fighting Cocks pub. From here the main route heads back along Godshill Ridge to reach Ashley Walk car park, passing Godshill cricket pitch. The route then descends to Millersford Bottom before climbing back up to the car park. Alternatively you can follow a longer loop passing through an area that, during WWII, formed part of the Ashley Walk Bombing Range. After crossing the Ditchend Brook the route visits Pitts Wood Inclosure before heading west back to the car park, passing Ashley Walk car park and Millersford Bottom on the way.

From Godshill Wood car park head north-east away from the road following a broad grassy path with a fence and trees to your left for 700m. Turn left through the gate (easily missed) and follow the path through the trees of **Godshill Inclosure**. Turn right along the gravel cycle track for 25m to a junction (SU 180 167, shared with Walk 3). Turn left and keep ahead along the gravel track through mixed woods for 700m. Where the track bends hard right (SU 173 169) go straight on along a narrower path to reach a small gate and leave the inclosure.

Turn right down the road towards Woodgreen for 50m and then turn left at the junction along the road for **Castle Hill**, now following part of the Avon Valley Path.

The 55km (34-mile) **Avon Valley Path** follows the River Avon from the cathedral city of Salisbury in Wiltshire, heading south through Hampshire to Christchurch Priory in Dorset.

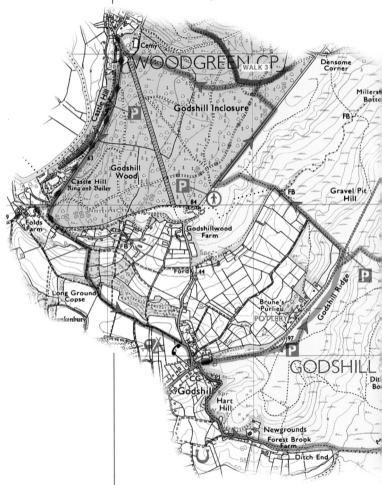

Continue along the road, passing a small car park to reach a second parking area at **Castle Hill Viewpoint** (SU 170 166). ▶

Continue alongside the road, using the verge where available and start descending. Follow the road round to the left (ignoring a track to the right) and soon fork right along a gravel track past Arden Lodge. At Brook Cottage, continue between the hedges and cross a footbridge to reach a fingerpost and path junction in the field. Turn up to the right, following the fence on the right past some trees, cross a stile in the top right corner and keep ahead through the trees to cross another stile. Head diagonally left up through the trees and turn left along the track to a house and track junction.

Turn right (south) along the hedge-lined track (this soon becomes just a wide path) for 350m to reach a path junction. Go straight on through the small gate and follow the enclosed path. Dogleg left over a stile and continue, now following the field boundary on your right. In the far right corner of the field ignore the track down to the gate but keep ahead to leave via the small gate in the corner. Turn right up the road to a T-junction with Roger Penny Way (B3078) next to the **Fighting Cocks pub** (SU 175 149).

Here you have a choice of continuing with the main walk or following the extension to Pitts Wood Inclosure.

Sit a while and admire the lovely view out across the River Avon towards Wiltshire.

35

Looking across Millersford Bottom towards Godshill Inclosure

For the main walk turn left towards Cadnam, keeping alongside the B3078 for 500m and when the road starts bending left, fork right along the gravel track into Godshill Cricket Pitch car park. Keep ahead onto the open grass area (cricket ground) and bear left, soon the path splits; keep to the left fork and follow a broad, grassy path between the gorse bushes, heading in a north-easterly direction roughly parallel to the road (B3078) to reach **Ashley Walk car park** (SU 186 156).

Continue alongside the road for a further 100m, then turn left across the road and pass a low vehicle barrier (the longer walk rejoins here). Follow a grassy path between gorse bushes, keeping the wire fence on the left, and then head steeply downhill with views over Millersford Bottom. Keep ahead with the fence and trees over to the left and cross the **footbridge** over Millersford Brook. Continue beside the trees (left) and then up over open ground, bearing diagonally left (west) after some trees to arrive back at the car park.

WALK 2 – GODSHILL AND CASTLE HILL

Alternative route

From the junction beside the Fighting Cocks turn left for 20m and then right, following the lane towards **Newgrounds** for 1km, keeping right at the split signed for Hartwell. On reaching a large barn at Fernlea Farm, fork slightly left onto a grassy path at the vehicle barrier, but still continue eastwards parallel with the lane. Keep ahead, following the trees on the right, to reach a ford over **Ditchend Brook**; crossing may be difficult if water levels are high. Continue straight on over open ground towards the trees.

Go into **Pitts Wood Inclosure** (SU 189 143), passing a small cast-iron plaque by the old gateposts.

The land here contains varying amounts of clay and **Pitts Wood Inclosure** was one of several sites in the Forest where Romano-British pottery kilns have been found. The iron plaque mentions that the wood was enclosed in 1775, thrown open in 1815 and then re-enclosed in 1903; the wood is no

Heading towards Pitts Wood Inclosure

A spider and its web on a dewy autumn morning at Godshill Ridge

longer enclosed. It's hard to imagine, but this area was once part of the Ashley Walk Bombing Range during WWII, where many experimental bombs were tested.

Follow the main track heading east through the wood for 800m, ignoring a track to the left, and keeping straight on at two crossing routes. At a skewed T-junction go straight on along a level path through the trees, keeping left at the split to reach a gravel track (alternatively, fork right up along the track to a cross-junction and turn down to the left).

Turn left downhill to cross a stream and keep straight on at the junction. The route now follows this gravel track for 2.1km (1¼ miles). From **Lodge Hill** there are good views down into Hive Bottom. Keep left at the junction heading west-north-west over **Cockley Hill** and down to cross a bridge over **Ditchend Brook** before climbing up to Ashley Walk car park. Turn right alongside the road (B3078) for 100m and then turn left across the road to a low vehicle barrier. From here, follow the directions given for the main route to return to the start at Godshill Wood.

WALK 3
Hatchet Green and Woodgreen

Start/finish	Deadman Hill car park (SU 192 165), on the B3078, 2.4km (1½ miles) east of Godshill
Distance	9.3km (5¾ miles)
Time	2¾hrs
Maps	OS Explorer OL22
Refreshments	The Horse and Groom (01725 510739) and village shop / tearoom (01725 512467) at Woodgreen – short detour

The walk starts from Deadman Hill and heads north across the open heath of Hale Purlieu towards Hatchet Green with its picturesque thatched cottages. It then passes Hale House and St Mary's Church, following a section of the Avon Valley Path. After having a quick look at the River Avon it's off to Woodgreen Common with its cricket pitch, where a short detour to the village shop or Horse and Groom pub in Woodgreen can be made. The final section goes through Godshill Inclosure before passing Densome Corner and dipping down to Millersford Bottom before a short climb back to the car park. There are a few stream crossings with no footbridges near Millers Ford which can require care after heavy rain.

Head north from the car park down a steep, stony path passing just left of a clump of Scots Pine. Cross a stream at **Millers Ford** and continue heading in a general north-easterly direction, with trees over to the left. On reaching the dense wood ahead, turn left and follow a meandering path through the trees as it bears right and then left to cross a stream. Go gently uphill through the trees and bear left at a junction to shortly leave the wood. Fork diagonally right to follow the broad stony path heading north-north-east over the open heath of **Hale Purlieu** for 1.1km (¾ mile), ignoring a crossing path and passing under the power lines. Heading slightly downhill, cross a stream and go left along a path, soon following the line of trees and fence on the right to reach a road (SU 194 187).

In 1257 the boundaries of the New Forest were extended to include the area that is now known as **Hale Purlieu**. However, the extension was short lived as the boundary was returned to its original line in 1280 and Hale Purlieu returned to being an adjacent common of the New Forest. The word 'purlieu' means an area that has been removed from the Forest and was no longer subject to Forest Law. Almost 700 years later the land was brought back within the Forest boundary under New Forest Act of 1964.

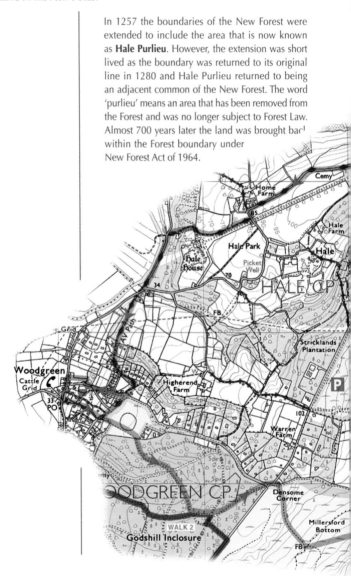

Cross the road and turn right, following the raised path on the left side of the road to miss a sunken section, before continuing along the road again (ignoring a bridleway to the left). At the right-hand bend, turn left along a track (bridleway) up towards **Hatchet Green**. At the village hall bear right through the car park and then go left along the surfaced lane towards a thatched cottage, The Old Dame School. To the right is the large village green and on the left is a stone sculpture and two memorial trees. ▶

The stone sculpture, by Paul Wilson, was commissioned to celebrate the Millennium, as was the planting of one of the trees; the other commemorates the 40th anniversary of Queen Elizabeth II's accession to the throne.

Turn right to a T-junction and then left along the lane for 1km, passing more thatched cottages, including The Old Post Office. The route is now following part of the Avon Valley Path (AVP). At **Home Farm** follow the lane to the left for 50m and then turn right through a gate at the footpath sign (SU 183 187), still following the AVP.

Keep close to the fence on the right; over to the left is the lime-tree-lined drive to **Hale House**. Cross a track and keep ahead before bending right near the house, cross another track and keep ahead down the surfaced path, passing **St Mary's Church** to reach Moot Lane. Before continuing with the walk, cross straight over Moot Lane and along the track for a few metres to reach the bridge and a peaceful view of the River Avon. ▶

The River Avon, which rises in Wiltshire, meanders its way through Salisbury and then along the western edge of the New Forest, joining the sea at Christchurch Harbour in Dorset.

The Palladian style **Hale House** was built by well-known London architect Thomas Archer in the 18th century. However, the manor of Hale dates back to at least the 14th century when Adam de

St Mary's Church at Hale

la Forde was granted a licence to hold services at the manor. St Mary's Church, which dates from the 14th century, although it was altered and enlarged by Thomas Archer, contains many memorials to former owners of the manor, the oldest being to Sir John Penruddock (d.1600) and the most striking to Thomas Archer (d.1743) and his two wives.

Turn left (or right if coming back from the river), following the AVP along Moot Lane, and bear right at the junction towards Woodgreen and Breamore for 25m, then go left up the drive towards North End. Cross the stile just to the right of the entrance gate and follow the field boundary on the right; to the right you can see Breamore House in the distance. Continue through three fields separated by stiles and then keep ahead along the gravel track, following it as it bears left. Keep right at the split to join a road at Woodgreen Common (SU 174 175). ◄ Here you can follow the pub/shop detour, which adds 700m, or continue with the main walk.

Notice the Avon Valley Path sign – it's 19.3km (12 miles) to Salisbury and 35.4km (22 miles) to Christchurch.

Pub/shop detour

Turn right down alongside the road and after a lane joins from the left follow a permissive path on the right-hand side of the road. Go through a gate and follow the enclosed path to reach the village shop and tearoom. Turn left along the road passing the village hall and keep ahead at the junction to the **Horse and Groom**. Keep left at the next junction for 75m and when a road joins from the right, turn left over a stile just before a driveway. Follow the enclosed path, then continue up the gravel drive to cross a stile by a gate. Turn left along the lane and then right, following a gravel track with houses on the right (SU 173 174) – now follow the main walk.

If not visiting the pub, keep straight along Brook Lane and, shortly after the lane on the right, turn left along a gravel track (SU 173 174) – the pub detour rejoins here. Where the track swings right continue straight on across the common, passing between the cricket pitch and the clubhouse to reach a gate in the fence on the

Thatched cottage at Woodgreen Common

Take a short detour across Moot Lane to see this peaceful view of the River Avon

right; go through this to enter **Godshill Inclosure** (SU 175 172).

Follow the path down through Godshill Inclosure, cross the stream to a junction and go straight on uphill , keeping left to reach a track at SU 179 168 (shared with Walk 2). Turn left and go straight over the gravel cycle track, following a path north-east through the trees to reach a small gate at the corner of the inclosure. Go ahead and turn right along the road for few metres and at the left bend – **Densome Corner** – go east along the track signed 'Wild Close only', passing the low vehicle barrier. Once level with the cottage (left) bear diagonally right (south-south-east) across the open grass and then down past some trees to a stream in **Millersford Bottom**. Cross the footbridge and head diagonally left (east) uphill (aiming to the right of the Scots Pine trees passed earlier) to arrive back at the car park.

WALK 4
Bramshaw Telegraph and Eyeworth Pond

Start/finish	Telegraph Hill car park (SU 228 166), near the junction of the B3078 and B3080 at Bramshaw Telegraph, or Fritham car park (SU 230 140)
Distance	10.5km (6½ miles) or 8km (5 miles)
Time	3hrs or 2¼ hrs
Maps	OS Explorer OL22
Refreshments	The Royal Oak, Fritham (023 8081 2606)

From Bramshaw Telegraph the route follows rides and tracks through Islands Thorns Inclosure, once home to some Romano-British pottery kilns, before climbing onto the open heath of Coopers Hill, once part of the Ashley Walk Bombing Range. Then it's through Amberwood Inclosure and out across Fritham Plain to arrive at the little village of Fritham and the 17th-century thatched Royal Oak pub. The walk then heads for Eyeworth pond, which used to provide water for the Schultze Gunpowder Factory, and passes Irons Well, a chalybeate spring, before going north over Homy Ridge back to the car park.

A shorter walk, missing out Coopers Hill and Amberwood Inclosure, is also described and a more open alternative route skirting round Islands Thorns Inclosure is also given.

Bramshaw Telegraph, one of the highest points in the New Forest at 128m (420ft), was the location of an optical shutter signal station using a signalling system developed in 1796 by Rev. Lord George Murray (1761–1803). The station, one in a series that linked Plymouth with the Admiralty in London, was used to send messages during the Napoleonic Wars.

Alternative route
For a more open route turn left along the B3078 for a few metres and then left past a low vehicle barrier to follow a gravel track for 2.8km (1¾ miles), keeping Islands Thorns

Inclosure to the left, rejoining the main walk at a junction on **Coopers Hill** (SU 209 147).

For the main route, head south-west from the car park across the open heath towards the trees. Pass some old gate posts and enter **Islands Thorns Inclosure**. After 50m, keep right at the split following a grassy ride down through the trees, gently curving to the left past the site of **Studley Castle**.

> **Islands Thorns Inclosure** was first enclosed in 1852 when the area was cleared and planted with oak and it is now one of the largest even-aged oak plantations in the Forest. Studley Castle was once a royal hunting lodge (c.1360), though little remains apart from some earth banks and ditches. The clay soils around here supported a thriving Romano-British pottery industry until AD400.

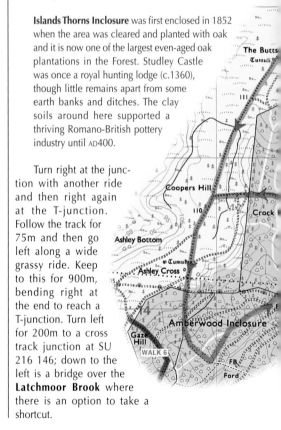

Turn right at the junction with another ride and then right again at the T-junction. Follow the track for 75m and then go left along a wide grassy ride. Keep to this for 900m, bending right at the end to reach a T-junction. Turn left for 200m to a cross track junction at SU 216 146; down to the left is a bridge over the **Latchmoor Brook** where there is an option to take a shortcut.

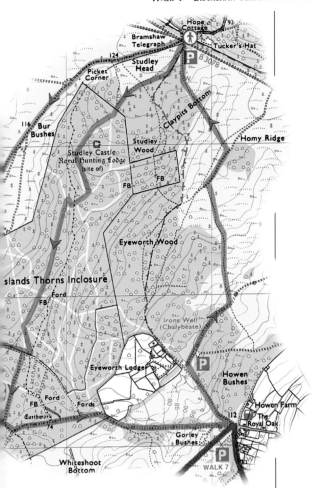

Shortcut

For a shorter walk keep straight on at the junction for
400m and turn left along the gravel cycle track to a
bridge over the Latchmoor Brook to rejoin the main
route.

The last remaining observation shelter from the former WWII Ashley Walk Bombing Range

For the longer walk turn right up the gravel track, ignoring any crossing paths and rides to reach the western edge of the wood on **Crock Hill**. Keep straight ahead over the open heath to a T-junction on **Coopers Hill** and turn left along a stony track (the alternative route comes in from the right here). After 500m the track passes a small brick shelter; continue straight on along the track towards the trees to reach a junction with a cycle track (SU 208 141).

The **brick shelter**, which is open on one side, is the last remaining observation shelter from the former WWII Ashley Walk Bombing Range. The range was used to test many of Britain's experimental bombs, including the 22,000lb (10,000kg) 'Grand Slam' designed by Sir Barnes Wallis, the largest bomb ever to be dropped in England.

First enclosed in 1815, most of the original oak plantation remains today.

Keep ahead through a gate following the grassy track down through **Amberwood Inclosure**. ◀

Cross over the track slightly to the right and go through the gate still following a grassy path downhill, now with a fence on your right. After 250m turn left along a grassy ride to reach a crossing track, keep straight ahead and then right (straight on) along a gravel cycle track, later bending right to cross a bridge over Latchmoor Brook (the shortcut rejoins the main route here). Follow the cycle track for 1.6km (1 mile) and bear left along the car park access track to join a road at Fritham (SU 231 141 – shared with Walk 7). ▶

Look out for the small black postbox in the trees on the left at the car park entrance, provided by the nearby gunpowder factory.

Fritham, first mentioned in the early 13th century, is a dispersed settlement of farms and houses situated in a large, oval medieval enclosure surrounded by forest and open heath. At one time it was a much busier place due to the nearby gunpowder factory.

To the right is the picturesque 17th-century thatched **Royal Oak**; however, we turn left down the lane to reach Eyeworth Pond.

Eyeworth Pond was created 1871 to provide water for the Schultze Gunpowder Factory at nearby Eyeworth Lodge which closed in 1921. Although gunpowder for sporting guns had been made here from 1859, it wasn't until Edward Schultze took over the factory in 1869 that large-scale production of smokeless gunpowder was started. At its height the factory employed about 100 people.

Eyeworth Pond – built to provide water for the former Schultze Gunpowder Factory

Irons Well – a chalybeate spring

This track was once used by the gunpowder carriers from the nearby factory.

Turn right to go between the pond and car park and continue straight on past the low vehicle barrier following the gravel cycle track. ◀ Shortly pass **Irons Well** on the left of the track – keep a lookout for the wooden fence around the rusty red-brown spring.

Irons Well is a chalybeate spring meaning that the water contains iron salts; the iron gives rise to the rusty orange-red colour. At one time the waters were believed to have curative properties for various ailments, including sore eyes and bad legs.

Continue along the track and on reaching the edge of the trees, turn diagonally left over the open ground to shortly cross a stream. Continue in a northerly direction up the wide grassy area, with trees of **Eyeworth Wood** to the left and some smaller stands to the right, to reach a gravel path at the top of the rise. Turn right, following the main path to reach a junction to the left of the trees at **Homy Ridge**. Turn left and follow the defined path downhill and, after crossing a stream, go uphill to the car park.

WALK 5
Bramshaw Church and Nomansland

Start/finish	Pipers Wait car park (SU 249 165), 3.1km (2 miles) west of Brook on the B3078 and then right towards Nomansland for 1.1km (¾ mile); alternatively, Bramshaw Wood car park (SU 257 173) or Shepherds Gutter car park (SU 260 152)
Distance	8.2km (5 miles)
Time	2¼ hrs
Maps	OS Explorer OL22
Refreshments	Lamb Inn, Nomansland (01794 390246)

From Pipers Wait, near the northern edge of the forest, the walk heads through Bramshaw Wood to pass the unusual Clock Tower House and Bramble Hill Hotel. A section of quiet road brings the route to Bramshaw and then across open farmland to pass a wood carpeted in bluebells in the early summer. The route follows another section of road before crossing open fields to reach St Peter's Church in Bramshaw. Then it's off through Bramshaw Wood again to reach the Lamb Inn at Nomansland from where it's a short hop back to Pipers Wait. Anyone wanting a pub stop halfway round the walk can start from Shepherds Gutter car park, which adds 800m (½ mile).

Alternative start

If starting from Shepherds Gutter car park, leave the car park and turn along the road, crossing **Shepherds Gutter** and continue beside the road to the entrance to **Bramble Hill Hotel** to join the main route. On completion of the walk, retrace the section from the hotel driveway back to the car park.

Start from Pipers Wait car park and head south-east across the open heath, keeping the trees of **Two Beeches Bottom** over to the left. Keep straight on at a crossing path and follow the path as it starts to curve left. At the split take the right fork heading towards the trees and start bearing slightly left to keep the trees to your right.

Soon the trees
come in from
the left;
continue
along

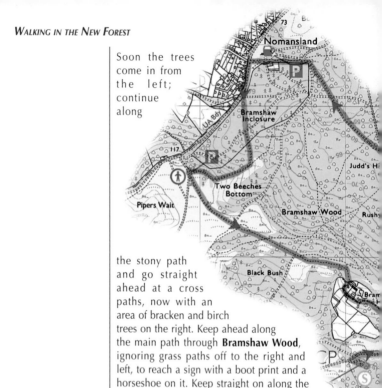

the stony path
and go straight
ahead at a cross
paths, now with an
area of bracken and birch
trees on the right. Keep ahead along
the main path through **Bramshaw Wood**,
ignoring grass paths off to the right and
left, to reach a sign with a boot print and a
horseshoe on it. Keep straight on along the
level bridleway for 350m; this can be muddy
in places and the parallel footpath, about 40m to
the left, can be used – this later rejoins the main route
at another sign facing the other way.

> **Bramshaw Wood** has a good mix of oak and beech
> and it's claimed that oaks from this wood were used
> in the construction of Salisbury cathedral during the
> 13th century.

At the split, fork right down past a large gate beside
a brick house (Peacock Cottage) to join a gravel track at a
corner (SU 260 158); on the left is the Clock Tower House.
Complete with clock tower, this was once the stable block
for the adjacent Bramble Hill Lodge (now a hotel).

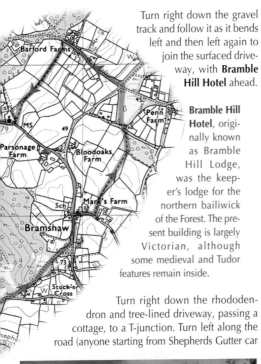

Turn right down the gravel track and follow it as it bends left and then left again to join the surfaced driveway, with **Bramble Hill Hotel** ahead.

Bramble Hill Hotel, originally known as Bramble Hill Lodge, was the keeper's lodge for the northern bailiwick of the Forest. The present building is largely Victorian, although some medieval and Tudor features remain inside.

Turn right down the rhododendron and tree-lined driveway, passing a cottage, to a T-junction. Turn left along the road (anyone starting from Shepherds Gutter car

The Clock Tower House beside Bramble Hill Hotel

park comes along the road from the right) and at the junction fork left up a narrow lane, passing to the left of the some houses. Continue down the lane and bear left along the B3079 road in **Bramshaw** for 150m.

Go right up the lane, passing the red-brick Wesleyan Chapel (dated 1883), and after the house on the left, turn left over a stile beside a gate and footpath sign. Follow the fence on the right, cross a stile and keep along the fence through the next field to another stile. Continue through the wood, keeping straight on at the marker post. ◀

In early summer the wood is carpeted in bluebells.

Leave the wood via the stile and go diagonally left between the garden fence and pond to join a gravel driveway (SU 272 166).

Head north across the open common, aiming for the white crossroad sign in the distance. Turn left along the road towards Nomansland for 500m, not the sharp left road to Bramshaw and Fritham. After passing some houses on the right, just before the brow of the hill, turn left over a stile beside the gate and footpath sign. Cross the track and over another stile on the left, then continue along the enclosed path. Cross a stile and follow the fence on the right through three fields separated by stiles. After crossing a stile by a large tree, with the churchyard visible ahead, go diagonally left down across the field. Pass the lower left corner of the churchyard and follow the brick wall to a stile and road (B3079) at SU 265 166. Turn right through the small gate and up the steps past **St Peter's Church** and then down the other side to leave via another small gate, missing out the narrow section of road.

St Peter's Church once marked the boundary between Hampshire and Wiltshire until the County of Southampton Act 1894; local folklore had it that half of the church was in one county and half in the other. The stone nave is early 13th century, whereas the rest of the church was rebuilt in 1829. Inside is a memorial to seven local people who were heading to America to start a new life, but sadly perished on the *Titanic*.

Proceed carefully down the road as it bends to the right and, just before the 40mph signs, fork left past a low vehicle barrier. Follow the wide grassy path through the trees heading north-west, ignoring a path off to the left and a crossing path, to reach a footbridge at a stream and boggy area. Go straight on, ignoring a path to the right, and over a crossing path. Continue uphill to reach Bramshaw Wood car park (SU 257 173) and turn left along the road towards **Nomansland**. Shortly on the right is the cricket pitch and a small brick and timber building, known as the Sacrifice Well. ▶

St Peter's Church at Bramshaw at one time marked the boundary between Hampshire and Wiltshire The Sacrifice Well is a memorial to those from the parish who served in two World Wars.

The cottages in **Nomansland** are on the western side of the road lying in Wiltshire and outside the forest perambulation, whereas the cricket ground is in Hampshire. It used to be known as 'no-man's-land' as the forest keepers had no jurisdiction over those who lived outside the boundary.

The Lamb Inn at Nomansland

At the T-junction, with the Lamb Inn ahead, turn left down the grassy area beside the road and at the bottom of the hill, where the roads bend slightly right beside a garage, turn left to pass a low vehicle barrier and enter **Bramshaw Inclosure**. Almost immediately turn right along a wide ride heading south for 200m to reach a junction. Go straight across, heading up through the trees and bear right up between tall beech and oak trees following a small ridge. At the split fork right through some Scots pine to reach Pipers Wait car park.

WALK 6

Abbots Well and Alderhill Inclosure

Start/finish	Abbots Well car park at Frogham (SU 177 128), 3.5km (2 miles) east of Fordingbridge
Distance	8.5km (5¼ miles)
Time	2¼hrs
Maps	OS Explorer OL22
Refreshments	The Foresters Arms, Frogham (01425 652294) – short detour

From Abbots Well car park the walk passes the old well before following tracks out across the open heath of Hampton Ridge with views across Latchmoor Bottom and later Alderhill Bottom. It's then off through the trees of Amberwood and Alderhill Inclosures, crossing the Latchmoor Brook and passing a memorial seat to the naturalist Eric Ashby. After a short rise up to Hasley Inclosure the route passes Little Witch and Great Witch, before dropping down to follow Latchmoor Brook to Ogden's car park. From here it's either a short climb back to the car park, or take a detour to the pub in Frogham.

Abbots Well, on the eastern edge of Frogham, was first recorded as Alleynewell during the reign of Edward I. The small spring has two parts – one brick-lined with a wooden lid and the other open for animals to drink from – and was for many centuries the main watering place for travellers along the old route to Southampton. Noted herbalist and author Juliette de Bairacli Levy (1912–2009), wrote *Wanderers in the New Forest* while living at a small cob cottage close to the car park. The book portrays an interesting picture of the New Forest, from the plants and animals to the forest gypsies and old farming practices. At the southern edge of the car park is an informative view indicator placed here to commemorate the Millennium.

Leave the car park and turn right down Abbotswell Road to the corner. On the way lookout for the small spring on the right.

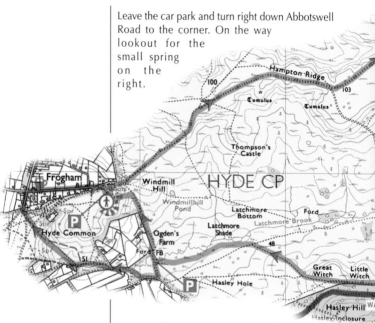

Keep straight on along the gravel cycle track, signposted for Fritham, for 2.9km (1¾ miles),

Looking towards Hampton Ridge from Windmill Hill – the walk follows the track into the distance

ignoring any side tracks and paths. Shortly after passing the trig point the route starts to head east along **Hampton Ridge**, with views to the right across Latchmore Bottom to Hasley Hill. ▶

Keep left at the split to continue along the main cycle track, heading north-east, and at the next split (SU 197 138) keep right. Shortly pass to the right of a small knoll and then a much smaller **tumulus** to reach a track and path junction near a small copse of oak trees (SU 203 141).

The area around here is a good place to catch sight of the rare Dartford Warbler.

The **knoll** to the left of the track conceals the buried remains of one of the targets, or 'submarine pens', used for the WWII Ashley Walk Bombing Range. There are several partially filled bomb craters surrounding the target: the largest, which is water filled, is about 50m to the south-west. The much smaller tumulus is the remains of a Bronze Age round barrow, or burial mound.

Turn right along a well-defined path, with **Alderhill Bottom** off to the right. Go straight over the crossing track and pass some wooden horse pens to enter Amberwood Inclosure. ▶

Follow the track down through the trees and keep ahead at the track junction, with deciduous trees to the left and conifers on the right. Keep to the track as it bends right into **Alderhill Inclosure** and ignore the crossing ride. About 100m after crossing a stream take the left fork at the split heading south. On the right at the path junction is a carved wooden seat. ▶ Continue along the track and cross the bridge over **Latchmore**

The inclosure, which straddles the Latchmore Brook catchment, was first enclosed in 1815 and most of the original oak plantation remains today.

This seat is dedicated to Eric Ashby MBE (1918–2003), naturalist and film-maker who lived nearby at Linwood.

59

Brook and through the gate to leave the Inclosure (SU 201 130).

Do not go through the gate ahead but turn right along the wide grassy strip, or driftway, between the fences of Alderhill Inclosure to the right and Sloden Inclosure to the left. Keep ahead to the end of the fence on the right to reach a path junction (SU 197 127). Turn left following a path up over the heather for 500m to reach **Hasley Inclosure**.

Turn right to follow the wide sandy path for 500m, with the fence and trees to the left. Pass the twin spurs of **Little Witch** and **Great Witch**, with views across Latchmore Brook to Hampton Ridge which was followed earlier. At the path junction on Great Witch fork right along the wide sandy path heading north-west, and keep to this path down to the valley. Do not cross the Latchmore Brook but turn left following the attractive tree-shaded stream along the valley, passing **Latchmore Shade** – a favoured spot for commoners' stock – to reach a gravel track at Ogden's car park (SU 181 123).

A lone tree near Hasley Hill

Here there is a choice of either heading directly for the car park or following a detour to the Foresters Arms in Frogham, which adds about 1km to the walk.

To return to the car park turn right and cross Latchmore Brook via the footbridge, follow the gravel track uphill for 400m, passing **Ogden's Farm**. As the fence and trees on the left end, keep straight on and at the next crossing path turn left up to the car park.

Latchmore Brook near Ogden's car park, a favoured place for commoners' stock to graze

Pub detour

From Ogden's car park turn left along the gravel track, go right at the junction and keep right at the split. Follow the left side of the track as it fords the stream and cross via a footbridge in the trees. Continue west along the surfaced track and, at the buildings on the left, fork slightly right, heading north-west up along a path over **Hyde Common**, keeping left of a white house and ignoring any crossing paths. Continue along the track and then road before going right at the crossroads along Abbotswell Road in Frogham; **The Foresters Arms** is on the left. Continue along the road to reach the car park on the right.

The Foresters Arms in Frogham

WALK 7
Fritham and Cadman's Pool

Start/finish	Fritham car park (SU 230 140), about 4.2km (2½ miles) north-west from the A31 at Stoney Cross, or Cadman's Pool car park (SU 229 122)
Distance	10.5km (6½ miles) or 8.5km (5¼ miles)
Time	3hrs or 2½hrs
Maps	OS Explorer OL22
Refreshments	The Royal Oak, Fritham (023 8081 2606)

Starting from the little village of Fritham, home to the charming 17th-century thatched Royal Oak, the walk heads out across the open heath of Fritham Plain and then through the deciduous woods to the south of Sloden Inclosure, passing the site of a former royal hunting lodge – The Churchyard. Then it's back onto open heath to cross Dockens Water at Splash Bridge before heading through Holly Hatch Inclosure to reach Cadman's Pool. The route then heads through South Bentley Inclosure, one of the oldest inclosures in the Forest, before arriving back at Fritham. A slightly shorter route via Holly Hatch Cottage, missing out Splash Bridge, is also described.

> **Fritham**, a dispersed settlement of cottages, farms, a small chapel and a picturesque 17th-century thatched pub, The Royal Oak, is situated in a large, oval, medieval enclosure surrounded by forest and open heath. The red-brick chapel was built in 1904 to replace an earlier 'tin tabernacle'. From around 1860 until the 1920s the Schultze Gunpowder Factory, which was based at nearby Eyeworth Lodge, employed many local people.

Walk south-west to the far end of the car park, pass a low vehicle barrier and continue along the well-defined gravel track across **Fritham Plain** for 1.5km (1 mile), passing over **Hiscocks Hill** on the way and ignoring all crossing routes. Shortly before the trees take the left fork at the split and immediately on entering the wood leave the

Splash Bridge over Dockens Water. A great place for lunch, this is passed on Walks 7 and 9

track as it bears left (this is the shorter route) and take the footpath ahead, with the fence of **Sloden Inclosure** to the right (SU 217 130).

Shortcut

After entering the wood at SU 217 130 keep left down along the track and later keep ahead across open heath. Shortly after the footbridge over **Dockens Water** bear right past **Holly Hatch Cottage** and, after 150m, turn left following the track south to a junction (SU 213 116) and turn left to rejoin the main route.

To continue with the main route walk keep along the level grassy path between large oak trees, later passing **The Churchyard**, once a medieval royal hunting lodge. ▶

Soon the path bears slightly left and starts to descend. Keep ahead and on leaving the wood you can see a broad track in the distance leading towards the trees of **Hasley Hill**. Keep along the path as it curves right and left. Bear left (straight on) along the gravel track for 600m,

All that remains of the lodge are the rectangular earth bank and ditch surrounded by yew trees.

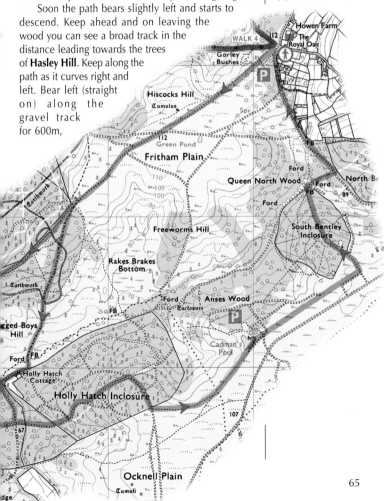

Holly Hatch Inclosure was first enclosed in 1810 around former pasture woodland, of which Anses Wood to the east is a remnant.

and just before a short rise turn left down a wide sandy path heading south-east (this is shared with the longer version of Walk 9).

Cross Dockens Water at **Splash Bridge** (SU 206 117), which makes a great place for a lunch stop. Keep ahead along the track, with the fence of **Broomy Inclosure** on your right. On reaching a broad gravel cycle track, with gate to the right, turn left for 600m through an area of oak trees planted in 1830. At the cross tracks at SU 213 116 (the shorter route joins from the left) keep straight on for 900m (the cycle track goes right), heading eastwards along the track up through **Holly Hatch Inclosure**. ◄

Ignore all side routes and where the track levels off next to a clearing (SU 221 119), turn right following a track south to leave the inclosure via a gate and reach **Ocknell Plain** (SU 223 117).

Cadman's Pool near Anses Wood was created by Deputy Surveyor Arthur Cadman in the 1960s to enhance the scenery

Turn left along the broad path, keeping left at the next junction. Continue along the concrete track to pass **Cadman's Pool** and reach a cross track leading to a car park. Cross over the track, pass a low vehicle barrier, and continue ahead for 750m, keeping parallel with the road to reach a crossing gravel track at SU 237 126.

The Royal Oak at Fritham is a picture-perfect thatched pub

This area was once part of the former WWII **Stoney Cross Airfield** (US Airfield AAF-452), which was operational between 1942 and 1946. The grassy strip and adjacent road formed part of the main runway (SW/NE 25/07). The three runways were later removed, though the outlines are still visible in aerial photographs.

Turn left along the track and through the gate, following the concrete track into **South Bentley Inclosure**, one of the Forest's oldest inclosures, dating from around 1700. At the far end of the concrete keep straight on along a path down through the trees. After passing a gate turn right to cross a stream at a **ford** – care is required here if water levels are high. Keep ahead through the open area before heading into the trees to reach a gate and fence.

Do not go through the gate but turn left, later leaving the trees to cross a bridge over the stream. Keep ahead along the path up the grassy area heading for Fritham, pass a low vehicle barrier and follow the track past Vale Cottage. Follow the lane passing the red-brick chapel and reach a junction with the **Royal Oak** ahead. Turn left and then left again along a gravel track back to the car park. ▶

On the north (right) side of the gravel track is a small black postbox which was provided by the nearby Schultze Gunpowder Factory to make deliveries easier for the postman.

67

WALK 8

Janesmoor Pond and the Rufus Stone

Start/finish	Janesmoor Pond car park (SU 247 136), between the A31 and B3078, east of Fritham, or Rufus Stone car park (SU 270 125)
Distance	8.8km (5½ miles); Salisbury Trench extension: 3.1km (2 miles)
Time	2½hrs (plus 1hr with extension)
Maps	OS Explorer OL22
Refreshments	Sir Walter Tyrell, Upper Canterton (023 8081 3170)

From Janesmoor Pond the route heads through King's Garn Gutter Inclosure, crossing Coalmeer Gutter via a ford to visit Upper Canterton and the Sir Walter Tyrell pub. After a quick look at the famous Rufus Stone the route meanders its way through woods to pass Lower Canterton. After a short section of road the route heads back through King's Garn Gutter Inclosure. For a slightly longer walk you can follow the loop through Salisbury Trench and the Coppice of Linwood.

Janesmoor Pond, starting point of Walk 8

Head south from the car park, with a fence on the left and **Janesmoor Pond** over to the right. Continue across the open grass dotted with gorse, keeping parallel with the road over to the right. Turn left along the gravel cycle track into **King's Garn Gutter Inclosure** and after 75m turn right, following a grassy ride as it descends and bends to the left. Ignore a path up to the left and keep ahead through a gate; a small stream is down to the right. Continue straight on to a junction of four rides and turn right for 100m, crossing a stream. At the next junction follow the ride to the left to reach a gravel cycle track (SU 256 131).

Turn right along the gravel cycle track and go through a large gate to reach a concrete track that goes off to the right up the slope. Turn left here, heading east across the open grassy area, and follow a path down through the open trees (there is also a parallel path which follows the fence on the left). The path becomes stony and reaches a ford at **Coalmeer Gutter** – cross using the concrete blocks. However, if it's flooded due to heavy rain the section to the Rufus Stone is best avoided by following the shortcut below.

Shortcut

Do not cross the stream, but head north along the grassy area between the fenced woods, following the fence on the left as it turns left to reach a gate at SU 263 134 and rejoin the main walk.

To continue the main walk, having crossed the stream, carry on across the open grassy area dotted with trees, heading in an easterly direction towards **Upper Canterton**. After a short time the **Sir Walter Tyrrell pub** comes into view (SU 268 127). This area can get rather waterlogged in the winter months.

Turn right along the road and just after the entrance to the pub car park fork left along a grassy track, passing a house and two low vehicle barriers. ▶ Turn right along the gravel drive to reach the Rufus Stone car park. Across the road, next to an oak tree, is the **Rufus Stone**.

To the left is a picturesque thatched house, Glen Cottage.

69

The **Rufus Stone**, covered by a three-sided cast iron pillar in 1841, is said to mark the spot where King William II, third son of William the Conqueror, was accidentally killed on 2 August 1100 by an arrow fired by Sir Walter Tyrrell. However, William II, commonly known as William Rufus because of his ruddy complexion, was an unpopular monarch and there has always been much speculation as to the exact circumstances of his death.

The iron-clad Rufus Stone said to mark the spot where William II was accidentally killed by an arrow fired by Sir Walter Tyrrell

From the back of the car park follow a path, roughly at right angles to the track from Glen Cottage. Continue down through the trees, heading north-east to reach a stream and ford paved with concrete 'sandbags'. After crossing the stream the path splits close to the fence corner on the right; take the left fork to reach a hedge on the left after 300m. Continue alongside the hedge through an open area, passing a low vehicle barrier to join a gravel track at Greys Farm in **Lower Canterton** (SU 277 130).

Keep ahead and then left at the track junction, following a signed bridleway past a house 'Woodpeckers'. Follow the fenced bridleway through the woods and go straight on along the surfaced lane to a T-junction. Turn right along the lane for 600m, on the way crossing a footbridge adjacent to a **ford**. Where the lane bends right fork left onto a hedge-lined gravel track.

Keep to the track as it curves left to head south, with a fence and line of trees to the left and **golf course** to the right. Cross **King's Garn Gutter** at the ford; if the water level is high go right for 25m onto the golf course and use the footbridge by the green. Once across the stream head diagonally right across

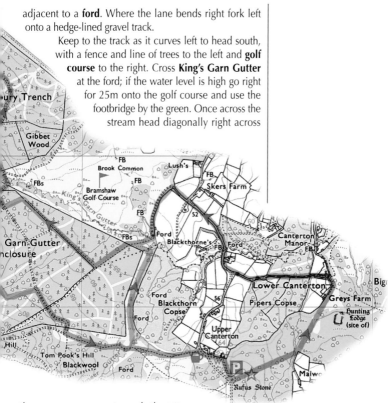

the open grassy area towards the trees, aiming for the small gate in the fence; the shortcut rejoins the main walk here (SU 263 134).

Follow the grass ride through the trees for 250m and turn right at a four-way junction to follow a gravel track for 400m. Where the track bends left keep straight on along the grassy ride; on the left is the old earth bank and ditch marking the boundary of Priors Acre.

Priors Acre, which now lies within King's Garn Gutter Inclosure, is one of the earliest enclosures,

71

dating from around 1700. Some remnants of pre-inclosure pasture woodland exist adjacent to the old boundary bank and ditch, which are still clearly visible.

Follow the ride as it bends left to join a gravel cycle track and turn right, then right again at the next junction, down through a gate into an open area (SU 254 138). Here there is a choice: either follow the main route back to the car park or follow the 3.1km (2-mile) extension through Salisbury Trench.

For the main route keep along the track for 60m and turn left up the grassy strip, or driftway, between the fenced woods, passing some wooden animal pens. At the end of the wood on the left turn left back to the car park.

Alternative route

Keep along the track and through the gate to a track junction. Turn right following the cycle track in an anti-clockwise direction through **Salisbury Trench** for 1.7km (1 mile) to reach a T-junction with another gravel cycle track (SU 247 147). Turn left, following the cycle track through the **Coppice of Linwood** for 900m.

The **Coppice of Linwood**, enclosed in the 1780s, has areas of older oak and beech especially near the streams. The adjacent Salisbury Trench is more recent and has a mix of oak, pine and beech dating from the 1930s, one of the few areas in the Forest with relatively extensive areas of this age of broad-leaf woodland.

Shortly after crossing the second stream (usually dry in summer) the track bends to the left. Fork right (almost straight on), following a ride through the trees, then keep straight on at two crossing rides. Shortly after crossing a small stream (again, usually dry in summer) go through a small gate and turn right up the grassy strip, or driftway, between the fenced woods. Turn left as the trees end to reach the car park.

Heading through King's Garn Gutter Inclosure

WALK 9

High Corner Inn and Ogden's Purlieu

Start/finish	Broomy Walk car park west of Stoney Cross; (SU 197 099)
Distance	5.2km (3¼ miles) or 9.2km (5¾ miles)
Time	1½hrs or 2½hrs
Maps	OS Explorer OL22
Refreshments	High Corner Inn, Linwood (01425 473973)

An easy, short walk or a longer alternative taking in Hasley Inclosure – the choice is yours. From the car park both routes head across Broomy Walk, with views to the west across to Ibsley Common, before descending to pass High Corner Inn and reach Dockens Water. Here the longer walk goes across Ogden's Purlieu and through Hasley Inclosure before crossing back over Dockens Water at Splash Bridge to reach Broomy Inclosure. The shorter, main walk takes a more direct route through oak and beech woods. Both routes then head up alongside Amberslade Bottom and across the open heath of Broomy Plain back to the car park.

Beautiful thatched cottage near High Corner Inn

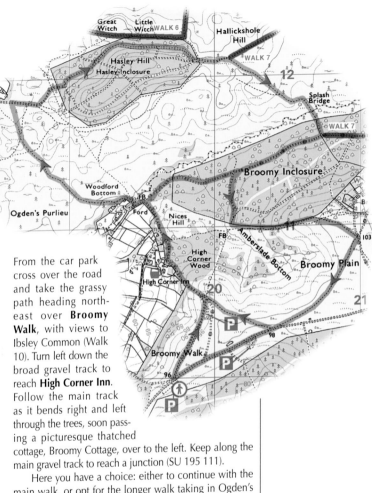

From the car park cross over the road and take the grassy path heading north-east over **Broomy Walk**, with views to Ibsley Common (Walk 10). Turn left down the broad gravel track to reach **High Corner Inn**. Follow the main track as it bends right and left through the trees, soon passing a picturesque thatched cottage, Broomy Cottage, over to the left. Keep along the main gravel track to reach a junction (SU 195 111).

Here you have a choice: either to continue with the main walk, or opt for the longer walk taking in Ogden's Purlieu and Hasley Inclosure.

For the main (short) walk turn right at the junction, passing a low vehicle barrier to follow the gravel cycle track. Go through the gate into **Broomy Inclosure** and continue along the gravel cycle track for 400m through the beech and oak woods to a track junction (SU 201

113) and turn right; the longer route comes in from the track ahead and turns left.

Broomy Inclosure, which was enclosed in 1829, has a mix of oak, beech and conifers. In early summer there is a good display of bluebells in parts of the wood.

Alternative route

At SU 195 111 turn left for a few metres and then right crossing the footbridge over Dockens Water at **Woodford Bottom**. Follow the main track as it curves left past Little Dockens and go past the low vehicle barrier heading east. Now follow the track diagonally out across **Ogden's Purlieu** heading west, with a large thatched cottage over to the left, and keep to the wide path as it starts to rise and head north-west.

Ogden's Purlieu is an area of sandy dry heath that was once under the control of Ogden Rooke in the latter half of the 17th century; a purlieu is land that has been removed from the jurisdiction of Forest Law, although it was later taken back within the perambulation of the Forest.

Looking north-west over Ogden's Purlieu

At a junction keep straight on up along a wide sandy path, keeping left at the split and go over the brow of the hill towards some gorse bushes. Fork right at the split and soon turn right along a stony track, ignoring a path off to the left through some Scots Pine. Keep to the main track as it curves left and right before passing a few more trees, and go through the gate into **Hasley Inclosure** (SU 189 119).

> The isolated, hill-top **Hasley Inclosure** which stands above the surrounding heath was planted in 1843 with oak, sweet chestnut, larch and pine. Only remnants of the original planting remain.

Fork left to follow the track in a clockwise direction through the northern half of the wood to reach a track junction near the eastern edge and turn left through a gate to leave the inclosure. Go straight on along the track and shortly turn right down a wide sandy path (shared with Walk 7). Cross Dockens Water at **Splash Bridge** (a great place for lunch) and keep ahead along the track, with the fence of **Broomy Inclosure** to the right. On reaching a broad gravel cycle track, turn right through a gate and follow the cycle track for 600m to a track junction and turn left (SU 201 113) to rejoin the main route.

For the main route, follow the track southwards for 250m and, at the left bend, turn right down a grassy track and leave the inclosure via the gate. Turn left up alongside the fence for 600m, with **Amberslade Bottom** to the right. Keep to the main track as it bears slightly right at the split, heading away from Broomy Inclosure to pass a wooden telegraph pole and reach a track junction next to the low vehicle barrier. Turn sharp right (not along the gravel cycle track) to head south-west along a curving grassy track across heather-clad Broomy Plain.

At the road turn right for 700m back to the car park. Alternatively, to avoid the road follow the grassy path north-west heading away from the road, cross over a gravel track and turn left retracing the outward route back over Broomy Walk to the car park.

WALK 10

Appleslade Bottom to Rockford via Ibsley Common

Start/finish	Appleslade car park (SU 184 092), 4.2km (2½ miles) east from Ellingham off the A338; alternatively, Blashford or Ellingham for anyone using public transport
Distance	9.7km (6 miles)
Time	2¾hrs
Maps	OS Explorer OL22
Refreshments	Red Shoot Inn, Linwood (01425 475792); The Alice Lisle, Rockford (01425 474700)

From Appleslade Bottom the route passes the Red Shoot Inn and through the dispersed hamlet of Linwood before crossing Dockens Water and heading over the open expanse of Ibsley Common, towards the western edge of the national park. The route then goes south along part of the Avon Valley Path through Mockbeggar and past Moyles Court to Rockford and The Alice Lisle pub. The final section meanders north-east over Rockford Common back to Appleslade Bottom.

The footbridge over Dockens Water at Linwood

From the car park turn right up alongside the road and at the junction next to the **Red Shoot Inn** (shared with Walk 11) turn left following the lane downhill. Keep to the lane as it bends right and continue along the gravel track through **Linwood**; fork left at the split following the gravel cycle track across Black Heath for 300m. Go left at the T-junction, passing a low vehicle barrier, and cross the footbridge over **Dockens Water** at SU 186 103.

Continue beside the fence on the right and keep ahead across the open heath for 150m to reach a path junction – it can get a bit wet here. Take the path diagonally left, heading south-west up through the heather to the ridgeline and continue in the same direction across Ibsley Common for 800m; soon the remains of some buildings can be seen over to the right. ▸ Keep straight on along the main path at a cross-junction to reach a **trig point**, a short distance to the right of **Whitefield Plantation**, a small wood of mature Scots pine. ▸

The ruins here include an air-raid shelter and octagonal brick structure, both associated with the former WWII airfield at Ibsley.

The trig point was adopted by the Ringwood and Fordingbridge footpath society in 1994.

> Now owned by the National Trust, **Ibsley Common**, along with Rockford Common, was originally owned by the Normanton family of Somerley Park just to the west of the River Avon. Scattered across the common are the remains of several Bronze Age burial mounds, or tumuli.

From the trig point head west along a path, descending slightly to cross a large, flat, grassy area dotted with gorse. At the far side go down a slope to pass a low vehicle barrier and join a track with a fence ahead (SU 166 098).

Turn left along the track towards **Mockbeggar** and keep right at the fork, passing to the right of Forest Holm. Ignore the stile and path on the right and keep straight on between the garden wall and fence. Fork left to follow the Avon Valley Path (AVP), passing to the left of some houses; the walk now follows this long-distance route for 2.1km (1¼ miles).

From the trig point near Whitefield Plantation the route heads west between gorse bushes

Bear right downhill following the AVP signs, cross the lane and continue across a small footbridge. Follow the path up some wooden duckboard sections, missing out a very muddy patch, and continue along the path with a fence to the right. At Newlands Plantation keep ahead through the kissing gate, and follow the enclosed path with fields to the right and a pine wood on the left. At the signed path junction turn right down the enclosed path (AVP) and go through gates either side of a farm track. Turn left alongside the road to pass **Moyles Court School** and a small parking area (this could be used as an alternative starting point).

The history of **Moyles Court** dates back to the Doomsday Book of 1086 when the land was held by Cola the

Huntsman. However, we need to jump forward several hundred years to the time of Dame Alice Lisle (1614–1685). Following the Battle of Sedgemoor in 1685, where the Duke of Monmouth's army was routed, Alice Lisle unknowingly gave refuge to some fugitives from Monmouth's defeated army. Unfortunately, they were discovered and Alice was arrested. The infamous Judge Jefferies found her guilty of treason and she was sentenced to be burnt at the stake.

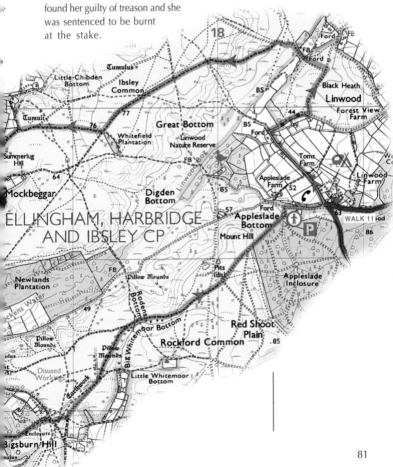

The ford and footbridge at Moyles Court

Notice the rather large oak tree on the left.

However, after the intervention of James II she was beheaded instead at Winchester on 2 September 1685. Alice is buried at St Mary and All Saints Church in Ellingham; the house is now a private school.

At the **ford** use the footbridge on your left to cross Dockens Water and turn right at SU 162 083. ◀

The oak tree, between the ford and the Linwood road, known as the **Moyles Court Oak**, is believed to be over 400 years old and the trunk is over 6.5m in girth. Just beyond the tree is the unusual site of a large sand bank at Rockford Pit, a former sand pit.

Head west along the road towards Rockford and Poulner with the stream to the right. At the junction for Ellingham go right for a few metres and then left over a metal stile.

Anyone using public transport could join the walk here having alighted at Ellingham, and followed the lane for 1.5km (1 mile).

The path splits; take the left branch (AVP) with a fence to the right running parallel to the road. Soon a lake can be seen through the trees on the right – one of several flooded former gravel pits. Cross the stile (the Avon Valley Path sign mentions it's 19.3km (12 miles) to Christchurch and 35.4km (22 miles) to Salisbury) and keep ahead

Donkeys waiting for opening time at the Alice Lisle pub at Rockford

83

along the verge. Over to the right is **The Alice Lisle pub**. Cross the cattle grid and keep ahead to the crossroads.

> The **Alice Lisle pub**, which occupies an 18th-century red-brick building that used to be Rockford village school, is named in memory of Alice Lisle from Moyles Court.

Anyone using public transport could join the walk here having alighted at Blashford, and followed Ivy Lane for 1.2km (¾ mile).

Turn left along the hedge-lined lane for 300m, curving to the right. Shortly after the houses on the left and right, turn left over a stile in the hedge and follow the path up across the middle of the field towards the trees on **Bigsburn Hill**.

Cross the stile (SU 165 078) and keep ahead through the oak trees, following the fence on the left. Go straight on across the track that leads to Chatley Wood House and at the T-junction go right along the track and then left, following the track as it bends to the right. Turn left at the next T-junction along a gravel track down a gentle slope, ignoring the track off to the left. Go up a slope and fork left past the low vehicle barrier.

Down to the right is the stream in Big Whitemoor Bottom.

Follow the level track. After 350m a track joins from the left; keep right as the track bears round to an easterly direction and ignore the crossing path. ◄ Fork right at the split (almost straight on), passing some trees to reach a track junction. Keep straight on over the open heath of **Rockford Common** and straight on at the next junction, heading in a north-easterly direction across **Mount Hill**. On reaching the corner of **Appleslade Inclosure** continue downhill, with the trees to the right, to reach the car park on the right.

WALK 11
Castle Piece and Linford Brook

Start/finish	Linford Bottom car park (SU 180 071), 4.4km (2¾ miles) east from the A31–A338 Ringwood junction
Distance	7.7km (4¾ miles)
Time	2¼hrs
Maps	OS Explorer OL22
Refreshments	Red Shoot Inn, Linwood (01425 475792)

From Linford Bottom the route follows tracks across the open heath of Rockford Common and Red Shoot Plain, before heading between Appleslade Inclosure and the broadleaved trees of Red Shoot Wood to reach the Red Shoot Inn. A short stretch of road leads to Amie's Corner and then it's along tracks to reach the easily missed remains of an Iron Age fort at Castle Piece. The final section is a gentle meander through Roe Inclosure to Greenford Bottom, a great place for a quiet picnic, and then alongside tree-shaded Linford Brook back to the car park.

From the car park head back to the road and turn right up past a couple of cottages to reach a track junction at the top of the rise. Turn right and take the left of the two tracks signposted for **Waterslade Farm**; the other is the cycle track leading down through Great Linford Inclosure. Follow the level track, with trees on your left and open ground on the right, for 500m. At the split fork slightly right past an old vehicle barrier and follow the track over the open heath – the trees on the left start to fall away. Keep ahead at a crossing path and continue in a north-easterly direction across **Rockford Common** (NT) with the trees of Red Shoot Wood over to the right.

Where the main path bends left to head north at SU 182 084, fork right (north-east), following a narrow path down towards the trees. Continue along the ride, with **Appleslade Inclosure** to the left and **Red Shoot Wood** to the right. Follow the old boundary line for 600m, ignoring paths to the right to reach a cross path junction (SU 189 089).

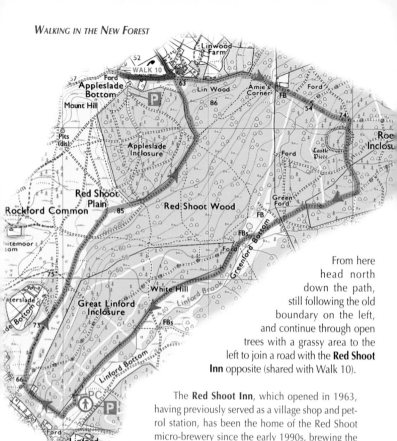

From here head north down the path, still following the old boundary on the left, and continue through open trees with a grassy area to the left to join a road with the **Red Shoot Inn** opposite (shared with Walk 10).

The **Red Shoot Inn**, which opened in 1963, having previously served as a village shop and petrol station, has been the home of the Red Shoot micro-brewery since the early 1990s, brewing the likes of Tom's Tipple, Muddy Boot and New Forest Gold.

First enclosed in 1811, Roe Inclosure offers a mix of broadleaved and coniferous woodland.

Continue along the road and at the left bend – **Amie's Corner** – bear right down a gravel track signposted for Roe Cottage. Go straight past the cottage and through the gate, following the gravel cycle track down through **Roe Inclosure**. ◄

Cross the bridge over **Linford Brook** at SU 196 091 and keep straight for 300m, heading gently uphill and ignoring a cycle track off to the left. Once the track starts

to level out a bit, look for a crossing path and turn right into the trees along a grassy path to shortly pass the easily missed remains of **Castle Piece**.

Modern art New Forest style – old tree roots in Roe Inclosure

> At **Castle Piece** are the remains of a small, circular fort, or enclosure, probably dating from the Iron Age (700BC–AD43). Being surrounded by trees it is quite difficult to identify the earth bank, the ditch having been almost completely filled in. However, the track does cut through the earth bank on the northern side and the rampart can be seen to the east of the path.

Follow the grassy path downhill and ignore the crossing path. ▶ Continue downhill to a junction with a gravel cycle track and ride opposite. Turn right along the gravel track, later ignoring a ride off to the right, to reach a gate (SU 194 083).

Notice the old earth bank crossing the path, the remains of a former inclosure probably dating from around 1700.

87

*Linford Brook at
Linford Bottom*

Leave Roe Inclosure and keep ahead along the track crossing Linford Brook via the bridge at **Greenford Bottom** – a great place for a rest or a picnic. Continue along the main track to a junction beside **Great Linford Inclosure**. Do not follow the cycle track through the gate, but stay outside the inclosure. Follow the path between the fence on the right and Linford Brook on the left for 1.6km (1 mile), passing through **Linford Bottom** to reach the car park; this section can get muddy after wet weather.

WALK 12
Exploring Bolderwood

Start/finish	Bolderwood car park (SU 243 086); follow the A35 from Lyndhurst for 4km (2 miles) and turn right along Bolderwood Arboretum Ornamental Drive for 4km (2 miles)
Distance	5.6km (3½ miles) or 9.2km (5¾ miles)
Time	1½hrs or 2½hrs
Maps	OS Explorer OL22
Refreshments	During the summer there is usually an ice cream van at the car park

The route heads through the trees of Bolderwood Walk to visit the Canadian Memorial and then heads south to North Oakley Inclosure. After crossing Bratley Water, which later joins the Lymington River, the route turns to head north through Bolderwood Grounds. Now following part of Radnor Trail, the walk passes the beautifully carved Radnor Stone and visits the deer viewing platform – where you might just catch sight of some fallow deer – before arriving back at the car park. A longer walk takes in more of North Oakley Inclosure before crossing Blackensford Brook and heading north to rejoin the shorter walk.

Head east from the Bolderwood car park, keeping left of the toilet block, and cross over the road to go through a gate opposite. Follow the track north-east down through **Bolderwood Walk**, ignoring rides to the left and right, and at the junction turn left along the gravel cycle track. Keep to the track as it bends right and left before going up a short rise to a T-junction.

Turn left along the gravel track and leave the inclosure by the gap next to the large gate (SU 240 093); just to the left is the **Canadian Memorial**.

The wooden cross at the **Canadian Memorial** was used for daily services by the troops of the Third Canadian Division who were stationed in the New Forest in the run up to the D-Day landings of 6 June 1944.

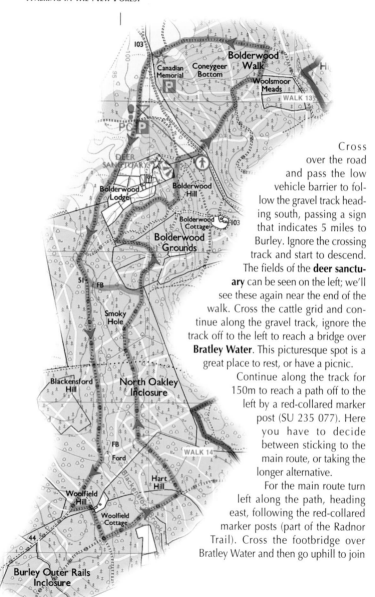

Cross over the road and pass the low vehicle barrier to follow the gravel track heading south, passing a sign that indicates 5 miles to Burley. Ignore the crossing track and start to descend. The fields of the **deer sanctuary** can be seen on the left; we'll see these again near the end of the walk. Cross the cattle grid and continue along the gravel track, ignore the track off to the left to reach a bridge over **Bratley Water**. This picturesque spot is a great place to rest, or have a picnic.

Continue along the track for 150m to reach a path off to the left by a red-collared marker post (SU 235 077). Here you have to decide between sticking to the main route, or taking the longer alternative.

For the main route turn left along the path, heading east, following the red-collared marker posts (part of the Radnor Trail). Cross the footbridge over Bratley Water and then go uphill to join

a broad gravel track and turn left (SU 239 077); the longer route comes in from the right.

The Canadian Memorial at Bolderwood

Alternative route

For a longer walk, at SU 235 077 continue south along the main track for 1.5km (1 mile) through **North Oakley Inclosure**. Later the track bends to a more south-westerly direction to reach a track junction at **Woolfield Hill**.

> **North Oakley Inclosure** was first enclosed in 1853 and planted with oak and beech. The original oak plantations remain along the valley beside Bratley Water, whereas areas of higher ground were later planted with Scots Pine and Douglas Fir.

Turn sharp left heading east towards **Woolfield Cottage**, and follow the track as it turns right to pass alongside the house which is now on the left. Keep ahead to reach a track junction in **Burley Outer Rails Inclosure**. Turn left for 600m, crossing **Blackensford Brook** to reach a track junction (SU 242 064).

*Track through North
Oakley Inclosure*

Turn left along the gravel track over **Hart Hill** and keep to the track as it heads northwards through North Oakley Inclosure for 1.5km (1 mile) to reach a junction with a path and a red-collared marker post, where you rejoin the main route (SU 239 077).

The main route continues along the gravel track as it bends right and left to reach a track junction and red-collared marker post in the trees of **Bolderwood Grounds**. ▶

Ignore the track off to the right and continue along the level cycle track as it curves left. At another red-banded marker post, turn right along a narrower track and fork left at the split (red and green collared marker post) with the open fields and **Bolderwood Lodge** to the left, passing through Bolderwood Arboretum. After 350m the track splits at a red-green collared marker post, fork right for 100m to reach a path junction by a wooden seat. Turn left and follow the gravel path up through the trees, soon passing the Radnor Stone which is to right of the path.

These were once the grounds of Bolderwood Lodge.

The engraved **Radnor Stone** is a memorial to the 7th Earl of Radnor, former chairman of the Forestry Commission and New Forest Verderer.

Continue up along the gravel path and shortly before the reaching the Ornamental Drive take the signed path to the left to visit the deer sanctuary viewing platform.

The **viewing platform** is a great place to see fallow deer at fairly close quarters, as they are fed here during the summer (Easter to mid September), usually early in the afternoon, though you may also see some deer here during winter and early spring. The informative notice boards give plenty of details about the five deer species that live in the Forest.

Follow the path up through the trees and cross the road to reach the car park.

WALK 13
Minstead and Furzey Gardens

Start/finish	Acres Down car park (SU 267 097), 2.7km (1½ miles) south of the A31 at Stoney Cross, or Minstead (SU 281 110), where there is a small car park beside the village green
Distance	8.7km (5½ miles) or 12.5km (7¾ miles)
Time	2½hrs or 3½hrs
Maps	OS Explorer OL22
Refreshments	Trusty Servant (023 8081 2137), village shop and tea room (023 8081 3134) at Minstead; farm shop and tea room at Acres Down (023 8081 3693)

From Acres Down the walk heads north along Ringwood Ford Bottom before turning east to follow quiet lanes to Minstead, resting place of Sir Arthur Conan Doyle and home to the unusually named Trusty Servant pub. It's then off along bridleways, passing Furzey Gardens with its colourful blooms, to reach Stonard Wood where you have a choice to make. Either opt for the shorter route heading south over Hart Hill or follow a longer alternative near to Highland Water before climbing up over Acres Down back to the car park. Either way, before leaving call in at Acres Down farm shop for a cream tea.

From the car park turn right along the track and then left at the junction, signposted for **Acres Down House**. After passing a white bungalow keep ahead over the open heath for 500m, passing just to the right of a stand of trees surrounding an old pit and then keeping alongside the edge of the trees on the right.

Where the path starts to bear left and climb slightly towards some tall conifers (SU 264 102), turn right down through some oak trees to cross a stream at **Ringwood Ford**. Once clear of the trees continue uphill heading in a north-easterly direction past clumps of gorse and birch; later the path levels off and passes through some holly bushes. There are several paths around here, which can be confusing, but the aim is to join a road opposite a small red postbox and entrance track to some houses at SU 267 105.

Cross over the road to the right of the track opposite and head along the left side of the small grassy area, passing an old vehicle barrier and bridleway sign. Continue into the trees and head downhill for 500m. Turn right along the surfaced lane and then left at the junction for 600m to a **ford**. Cross the Fleetwater using the footbridge and turn right onto a track for a few metres and then left through a kissing gate, following the signed path up through the wood for 400m, later enclosed, to reach a surfaced lane beside **All Saints Church**; to visit the church turn right through the lychgate.

Take a look inside **All Saints Church** to see the 17th-century three-decker pulpit and the font, which is believed to be pre-Norman. It is carved with four religious scenes: the Lord's baptism (west); the Lamb of God (east); lion with two bodies (north); and two eagles and a tree (south). The

All Saints Church at Minstead dates back to the 12th century

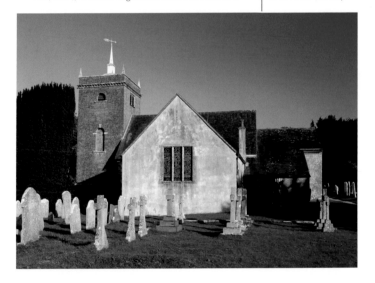

churchyard is the resting place of Sir
Arthur Conan Doyle,
creator of
Sherlock

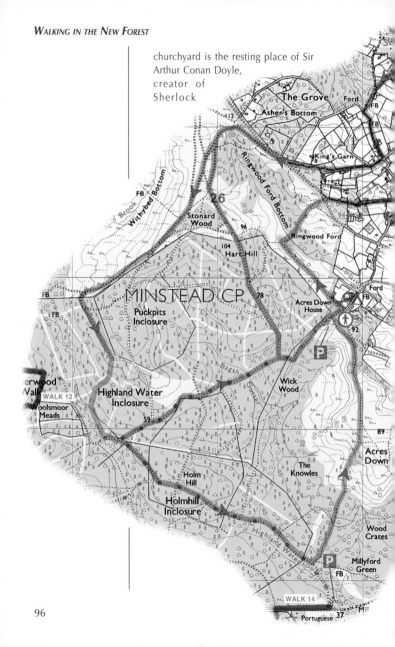

Holmes, the famous fictional detective – look for the tall stone cross under an oak tree to the south of the church.

Head down the lane, passing the old Technical School Building on the left, now Crofton Cottages, to reach the village green in **Minstead**. The Technical School was built in 1897 to commemorate the 60th year of the reign of Queen Victoria. Pupils were taught practical subjects such as laundry and woodwork.

Turn left along the road past the **Trusty Servant** and keep straight on, ignoring side roads. About 20m after the turning to Newtown and Fleetwater go right onto an enclosed path running parallel to the road to bypass a narrow section of road, and then keep ahead alongside the road for 125m. Turn left at the footpath sign and stile next to the large gate and continue through the field to a stile in the lower right corner. Cross the footbridge and

The gravestone of Sir Arthur Conan Doyle (creator of fictional detective Sherlock Holmes) in All Saints churchyard, Minstead

The Trusty Servant, village green and stocks at Minstead

PICTURESQUE MINSTEAD

Picturesque Minstead, known as Mintestede (the place where mint grows) in the Domesday Book, has a village green complete with replica stocks, some thatched cottages and a pub (the Trusty Servant), village shop and tea room. The sign at the Trusty Servant is a copy of the original painting of the Trusty Servant from Winchester College; the accompanying 16th-century saying probably originates from the days when pupils had personal servants:

… The porkers snout not nice in diet shows, the padlock shut no secrets he'll disclose, patient the ass his masters wrath will bear, swiftness in errand the staggs feet declare, loaded his left hand apt to labour saith, the vest his neatness open hand his faith, girt with sword his shield upon his arm himself and master he'll protect from harm.

The Trusty Servant pub sign at Minstead is a copy of the original painting at Winchester College

keep ahead through the next field to a stile in the top right corner, turn right along the lane and then left at the junction, soon fork left into the car park at **Furzey Gardens** (SU 273 115).

The informal **Furzey Gardens**, surrounding a restored 16th-century thatched forest cottage, were established in 1922 and are renowned for their year-round colour, including a dazzling display of azaleas and rhododendrons (023 8081 2464; **www.furzey-gardens.org**).

Continue through the car park, passing the garden entrance, and continue along the waymarked track. At the split keep to the right fork, following a path down through the trees to reach a kissing gate. Turn left and shortly after crossing a footbridge follow the path left to a stile and continue along the enclosed path to reach a lane. Turn right up along the track passing The Red House, keep right at the split to pass a house – **King's Garn** – and soon fork right again to reach the road (SU 264 107).

Cross over and turn right following a path parallel to the road, at the entrance to Heath House (on the right), follow the path bearing slightly left away from the road and later turn left along a defined track to reach a split by some trees (SU 260 109); here you have to decide between the main route or the longer alternative walk.

For the main route, fork slightly left, passing through some trees and then left again along a wide stony path, with **Stonard Wood** on your right to reach a trig point on **Hart Hill**. Continue down the track to reach a wooden seat with memorials to several members of the Burnett family, heed the saying on one: *O sit still, and look long, and hold yourself quiet*. Continue downhill, keeping straight on at two track junctions before going up a short rise to a T-junction and turning left along the gravel cycle track to reach the car park.

Alternative route

From the split in the track at SU 260 109, fork slightly right, staying just right of the trees, ignoring any side tracks and keeping **Stonard Wood** to your left. Follow the track downhill, ignoring the track into Puckpits Inclosure and, at the second track by a large beech tree, turn left past a gate and follow the level track through **Highland Water Inclosure** for 450m. Where the track bears left, turn right down a grassy ride, ignore rides to the left and right and keep left at a fork to reach **Highland Water**. Follow the ride parallel to the stream to join a track just left of a bridge (SU 252 089).

Turn left along the track for a short distance to reach a track junction. ▶ Keep right, passing a gate, and follow the track for 1.5km through **Holmhill Inclosure** to reach a gate.

Continue ahead for a few metres and, as the track curves right, bear left following a meandering path up through the trees, later climbing more steeply over **Acres Down**. ▶ After 1.6km (1 mile) pass a low vehicle barrier; do not join the track ahead but instead bear left (north-west) on a path through the trees. Follow any of the several paths over the brow of the hill and descend to the car park.

If time is short you can follow the track to the left for 1.7km, crossing **Bagshot Gutter** to head back to the car park.

From here there are good views out over the Forest.

WALK 14

Portuguese Fireplace and the Knightwood Oak

Start/finish	Millyford Bridge car park (SU 267 078), 3.4km (2 miles) west from Lyndhurst
Distance	9.7km (6 miles)
Time	2¾hrs
Maps	OS Explorer OL22
Refreshments	None on the walk, plenty of options in nearby Lyndhurst

From Millyford Bridge car park the walk passes the Portuguese Fireplace and then heads through the inclosures of Holiday Hills and Wooson's Hill. Then it's off through the beech trees of Mark Ash Wood, crossing the Bolderwood Arboretum Ornamental Drive to Anderwood Inclosure. The final section goes though the Knightwood Inclosure passing the famous Knightwood Oak – possibly the largest oak in the forest – before heading for Millyford Bridge via the Reptile Centre where you might be lucky and catch a glimpse of some of Britain's native reptiles.

From the car park head back to the road, cross over and turn right, walking parallel to the road to reach the **Portuguese Fireplace**.

> The **Portuguese Fireplace** is all that remains of a hutted camp that was occupied by a Portuguese army unit during WWI. The troops, working within the Canadian Timber Corps, helped the local labour force to fell timber for the war effort. The fireplace formed part of the cookhouse.

Mark Ash Wood

Church Moor

Hart Hill

WALK 12

Anderwood Inclosure

The Portuguese Fireplace near Millyford Bridge – all that remains of a WWI camp

Keep ahead parallel to the road for a short distance and turn left through the gate, heading south along the track into **Holidays Hill**

Inclosure. After 100m turn right along an undulating path through the trees for 600m, later bearing left to join a track. Turn right and follow the track into **Wooson's Hill Inclosure**; where the track bends left keep straight on along a path through the trees and turn right at a junction to leave the inclosure through a gate (SU 252 075).

This is probably the largest beech wood in the Forest.

Keep ahead for 25m and then turn left along a grassy track, descending to cross a bridge before rising up through the trees of **Mark Ash Wood**. ◀ Pass a low vehicle barrier and cross straight over **Bolderwood Arboretum Ornamental Drive** (SU 247 071) to pass another vehicle barrier. Follow the track downhill and just before the gate turn left on a woodland path meandering through the beech trees for 400m to reach a gate. Continue down through **Anderwood Inclosure** to reach a crossing track (SU 246 064).

On the way you will pass some smaller oak trees, including the Queen's Oak, planted by HM The Queen in 1979 to mark the ninth centenary of the New Forest.

Turn left along the gravel cycle track for 900m, passing a gate and ignoring rides to reach a track junction near **Winding Shoot**. Turn right, leaving the cycle track, following the track to the east through **Knightwood Inclosure** and, after 300m, follow the track to the right and then left. At the cross junction go right for 200m before turning left to follow a track to Knightwood Oak car park at SU 263 063 (this could be used as an alternative start). Follow the signs for the **Knightwood Oak**, crossing over the road to reach the famous tree. ◀

The **Knightwood Oak** is claimed to be one of the largest and oldest oak trees in the Forest, at 7.5m girth and around 600 years old. The tree is a great example of the ancient art of 'pollarding', the traditional way of harvesting wood without killing the tree. A pollarded tree is one where the upper part of the tree (above the reach of animals) has been cut back, promoting outward growth of fresh branches rather than the single main trunk continuing upwards. This greatly increased the yield of timber from the tree. However, pollarding of oak trees in the Forest was made illegal in 1698 as the timber

The famous Knightwood Oak – a typical pollarded oak tree, said to be the oldest in the Forest

from pollarded trees was no good for shipbuilding, which required long, straight trunks.

After admiring the tree, follow the looped path back to the road and turn right for 50m before turning right along a path (ride) through the trees for 700m, crossing a small stream on the way. Later a track joins from the left (SU 264 071).

Just before a large gate turn right following a path, which can be muddy in places, through the woodland, keeping parallel with the fence on your left. On joining a track with a house in front, turn left to pass the **New Forest Reptile Centre** (car park and toilets).

Sign for the New Forest Reptile Centre at Holidays Hill Inclosure

At the **New Forest Reptile Centre** you might be lucky and see some of Britain's native reptiles, including adders, smooth snakes and sand lizards, as well as frogs and toads which are housed in separate open air netted pens (open daily April to September).

Continue along the gravel cycle track through Holidays Hill Inclosure, keeping right at the junction to pass a gate. Turn right alongside the road, retracing the outward route back past the Portuguese Fireplace to the car park on the left.

WALK 15
Bank and Gritnam

Start/finish	Small parking area (SU 288 067), just west of the cattle grid on Pickney Lane between Lyndhurst and Bank at the corner of Brick Kiln Inclosure
Distance	7.6km (4¾ miles)
Time	2¼hrs
Maps	OS Explorer OL22
Refreshments	Oak Inn, Bank (023 8028 2350)

This short walk takes you through the beautiful ancient and ornamental woods to the south-west of Lyndhurst. First, the route heads southwards through Brick Kiln Inclosure and passes Butts Lawn before going through Hursthill Inclosure. Then it's alongside Highland Water through the beech and oak trees of Brinken Wood, before following indistinct paths at times to reach the little hamlet of Gritnam. From here it's a short hop to the Oak Inn at Bank before heading back to the car park.

At the small car parking area, stand with your back to the road and turn left through a small gate at the corner of the fence. Go diagonally left through the trees, heading east, and turn right along the gravel cycle track; the route now follows this main track gently down through **Brick Kiln Inclosure**. At the southern edge of the inclosure, go through the gate and keep ahead over **Butts Lawn**. Keep to the main gravel track as it curves right and continue for 300m to reach a track junction (SU 291 054).

Follow the track slightly to the right and go through the gate to enter **Hursthill Inclosure**. Note the sign indicating that this is a wildlife conservation area; dogs must be on leads and avoid disturbances. Follow the gravel cycle track for 200m heading west and turn right at the cross-track junction heading north, soon crossing a bridge over a stream. Keep to the track as it bends left with a ride to the right and keep to the track as it slowly turns to the left, heading west and then south over **Hurst Hill**.

Footbridge over Highland Water in the beautiful Ancient and Ornamental Brinken Wood

The meandering Highland Water becomes the Lymington River from Brokenhurst on its way to join the Solent.

Keep to the track as it turns left again to head east and arrive at a T-junction. Turn right down the cycle track and soon go through a gate leaving the inclosure. Continue along the gravel track, with trees to the left and a large grassy area to the right (a good place for seeing deer), to reach a bridge over **Highland Water** (shared with Walk 16) (SU 284 048).

Immediately after crossing the bridge turn right on a narrow path through the trees, keeping parallel with Highland Water and passing a deer-watching platform. ◄

Soon the stream splits; continue for a few metres then turn right over a footbridge, and follow the path through the trees heading north-west. After around 300m the stream comes back in beside the path from the right. Continue along the riverside path for 800m through **Brinken Wood** to reach a large footbridge at SU 276 060.

Brinken Wood is a beautiful example of the ancient and ornamental woods that the Forest has to offer, with a mix of beech and oak. Alongside the stream there are several good places for a picnic, or a quiet sit.

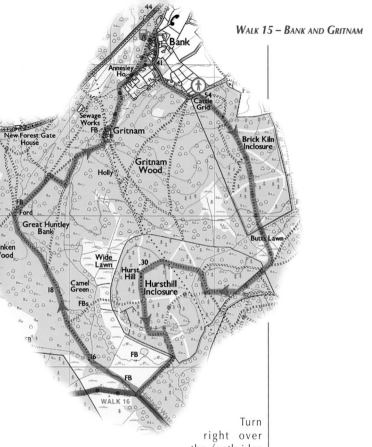

Turn right over the footbridge and follow the path through the trees, heading in a north-easterly direction for 350m to reach a faint path-crossing in a small clearing – ahead the path soon starts to rise gently. Be alert – the junction is easily missed. ▸ Having located the path junction (SU 278 062), turn right to follow the indistinct path through the trees for about 100m to a T-junction, with a small stream beyond. Turn left along this more defined path, keeping the stream over to the right. Soon bear right to cross the stream and continue through the trees heading

If you miss the cross path, just continue along the path and, at the small water treatment plant on the left, turn right through the trees to a track at Gritnam.

A frosty morning near Gritnam

north-east towards the houses of **Gritnam**, which can soon be seen through the trees.

Follow the surfaced track round the little hamlet of Gritnam in either direction as both routes join together just north of the houses. Then head north along the surfaced track towards **Bank**, keeping left at any splits, to reach the **Oak Inn**. Turn right just after the pub, following the lane down between the houses, before going uphill and bending left to reach the parking area.

WALK 16
Ober Water and Blackwater Arboretum

Start/finish	Whitefield Moor car park (SU 273 026), 3.2km (2 miles) west of Brockenhurst off the A337
Distance	11.7km (7¼ miles) or 6.8km (4¼ miles)
Time	3¼hrs or 2hrs
Maps	OS Explorer OL22
Refreshments	None on walk, plenty of options in nearby Brockenhurst. In summer there is sometimes an ice cream van at Whitefield Moor car park and Blackwater car park

From Whitefield Moor car park the route heads over open heath, with views of Rhinefield House, and then goes north through mixed woods to reach Blackwater Arboretum – a good place for lunch. Then it's on to visit two giant Redwood trees before crossing over the Rhinefield Ornamental Drive and following tracks to reach Highland Water. From here it's a gentle meander through the peaceful Queen Bower woods before following Ober Water back to the car park. There is one ford crossing over Black Water that may be difficult after heavy rain; however, a short detour is included in the route description and a much shorter alternative walk is also described.

From the car park turn left along the road for 75m and then right at two short wooden posts, following a path

Birch Bracket Fungus (piptoporous betulinus), also known as birch polypore or razorstrop, growing on a silver birch tree

south-west across the open heath for 700m. Ignore paths
to the right and left to reach a split immediately after crossing a raised gravel causeway through a boggy area. Fork
right, heading north-north-west, and cross another gravel
causeway beside **Silver Stream**. Continue along the broad

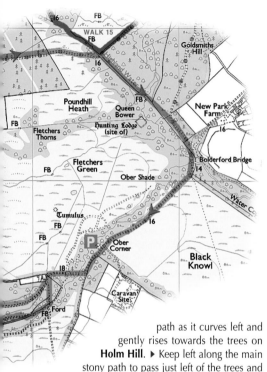

path as it curves left and gently rises towards the trees on **Holm Hill**. ▸ Keep left along the main stony path to pass just left of the trees and fork slightly right at the split to reach a path junction. Turn right downhill heading in a north-easterly direction for 800m, passing two stands of pine trees to cross a footbridge in some trees and keep ahead.

In the distance to the right is Rhinefield House Hotel.

Go through the gate into **Clumber Inclosure** (SU 264 032) and follow the ride to a cross junction (SU 263 033); here you can opt for the shorter, alternative route, or continue with the main walk.

Shortcut

Turn right along the ride and then right again at the T-junction to reach a gate. Cross straight over the road and past the low vehicle barrier, following the track ahead through **Aldridgehill Inclosure** for 1.4km (1 mile) to reach a white house, Aldridge Hill Cottage. Turn sharp right just before the gateway, passing a small iron plaque, and follow the main route from SU 281 033.

For the main route, continue straight on and shortly go through a large gate. Keep ahead across the grassy area with **Rhinefield House** to the right.

> **Rhinefield House** was built in the 1880s after the estate was acquired by the Walker family, who once owned Eastwood Colliery in Nottinghamshire, an area immortalised in the novels of D H Lawrence. The house displays a mix of Tudor and Gothic architecture, with battlements and mullioned windows. Inside, one room is modelled on Westminster Hall and another on the Alhambra Palace in Granada. Following substantial death duties in the 1950s the estate was sold and became a hotel in the 1980s.

Go through another gate and keep straight on with a fence on the right. At the fence corner go right for a few metres and then left along a ride for 350m, heading north-west away from the buildings, to reach a high fence. Turn sharp right alongside the fence, following it as it turns left to a track junction. Continue straight on along the gravel cycle track to reach **Black Water**. The ford crossing should not cause problems unless there has been heavy rainfall. The water normally passes under the concrete; if it's impassable follow the detour below.

Detour
Retrace the route to the track junction and turn left, turn left along the road by Rhinefield Cottage, soon crossing the bridge over Black Water. Just after the car park entrance turn left along a gravel track for 30m towards Blackwater Arboretum and then right onto a gravel path, rejoining the main route at SU 267 047.

After crossing the ford, continue north along the gravel track for 350m, ignoring a crossing ride, to reach a track junction. Turn right and keep ahead through a gate to enter **Blackwater Arboretum**.

Entrance gate to Blackwater Arboretum

> **Blackwater Arboretum** houses a small collection of trees, as well as a 'sensory trail' that encourages you to touch, smell and listen to some of the trees. There are also several picnic tables, making it a great place for lunch.

Having admired the trees, continue east along the track, leaving the arboretum, and shortly before reaching **Rhinefield Ornamental Drive** turn left along a gravel path (SU 267 047) through the trees, keeping parallel with the road – this is part of the Tall Trees Trail (across the road is Blackwater car park with toilets). Soon the path passes a sign by some coast redwoods and after 250m the path reaches a crossing ride and to the left are two huge redwood trees on either side of the ride.

113

GIANT REDWOODS

These two giant redwoods (*Sequoiadendron giganteum*), also known as Wellingtonia or giant sequoia, measure 55m, making them the tallest trees in the Forest. Native to America, giant redwoods can be identified by their thick, fibrous and rather spongy reddish brown bark and dark ever-green scale-like leaves pressed against the twigs. These trees on Rhinefield Ornamental Drive were planted in the 1850s, along with the Douglas firs and other redwoods, including coast redwood (*Sequoia sempervirens*). The coast redwood has similar bark to the giant redwood; however, the needles are about 15mm long on a flat plane from the twig, forming a feathery spray. Douglas firs have a furrowed bark, with soft needles and a fragrant smell.

Two giant Redwoods (*Sequoiadendron giganteum*), the tallest trees in the Forest

Turn right to cross Rhinefield Ornamental Drive and follow a slightly overgrown ride diagonally left through the trees, heading north-east to join a gravel track at a bend (SU 268 051). Turn right for 700m to a junction of four tracks and a ride, then turn left following the gravel track through **Poundhill Inclosure**. Go through the gate and continue along the track over the open heath to reach a bridge over **Highland Water** (shared with Walk 15) at SU 284 048.

Do not cross the bridge, but turn right just before it, following a path through the trees of **Queen Bower** wood, keeping parallel with the stream on the left and on the way crossing a footbridge and passing a wooden seat. ▶ Continue straight on to reach a gravel cycle track then turn right, crossing the Lymington River at **Bolderford Bridge**. Follow the track along the edge of **Black Knowl** heath and go straight on along the road at **Ober Corner** for 200m. Turn right along the track for Aldridge Hill caravan park and campsite and keep straight on towards a white house, Aldridge Hill Cottage (SU 281 033).

Turn left along a gravel track just before the house and after 25m fork left onto a path beside a small metal plaque. ▶ (The shortcut rejoins here.)

Follow the path south through the trees of **Aldridgehill Inclosure** to reach **Ober Water** – do not cross, but turn right alongside it (red trail). The path soon doglegs into the oak trees for a while and then continues alongside the stream. Ignore the footbridge to the left (yellow trail – which also leads to the car park) and keep ahead through a mix of holly, birch and Scots pine to reach **Puttles Bridge** car park. Turn left along the signed path to cross the footbridge over Ober Water and continue along the gravel path to the car park.

This is a great place to sit and admire the woods.

The cast iron plaque explains that Aldridge Hill was enclosed in 1775 and again in 1809, thrown open to the forest in 1843 and then re-enclosed in 1903.

WALK 17
Holmsley Walk and Burley

Start/finish	Holmsley car park (SU 221 011), 2.8km (1¾ miles) south-west of Burley
Distance	9.7km (6 miles)
Time	2¾hrs
Maps	OS Explorer OL22
Refreshments	Queens Head (01425 403423), Burley Inn (01425 403448), tea rooms and shops at Burley

The route leaves Holmsley car park and heads west along Holmsley Walk, before descending to pass Whitten Pond and cross the course of the old Southampton and Dorchester Railway. After passing Long Pond the walk heads across open heath to climb up to the remains of an ancient hill fort on Castle Hill. Then it's off to see Burley, home to several tea rooms, pubs, souvenir shops, a church and New Forest Cider. The final section descends Turf Hill before crossing the old railway at Holmsley Passage back to the car park.

From the car park turn left along the road for 40m and then right past a vehicle barrier. Follow the broad track for 1.2km (¾ mile), later passing an old quarry on your left. As the track starts to descend, bear right at the split, following the narrower path heading west – soon **Whitten Pond** comes into view. Follow the path passing to the left of the two ponds and then bear right, heading north; after 250m fork left to join the road just south of a bridge (SU 201 017).

For more about the railway see Walk 18.

Turn right, crossing the bridge over the former **Southampton and Dorchester Railway**. ◄ A few metres after passing the entrance to Burbush Hill car park turn left across the road to join a wide grassy path and immediately fork diagonally right onto a narrower path between gorse bushes. Continue through the heather, heading north-north-west to pass to the right of **Long Pond** and through some trees.

Long Pond passed on the way to Castle Hill

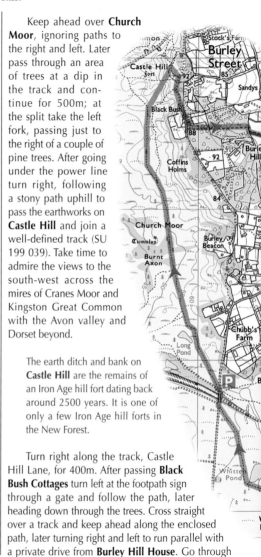

Keep ahead over **Church Moor**, ignoring paths to the right and left. Later pass through an area of trees at a dip in the track and continue for 500m; at the split take the left fork, passing just to the right of a couple of pine trees. After going under the power line turn right, following a stony path uphill to pass the earthworks on **Castle Hill** and join a well-defined track (SU 199 039). Take time to admire the views to the south-west across the mires of Cranes Moor and Kingston Great Common with the Avon valley and Dorset beyond.

The earth ditch and bank on **Castle Hill** are the remains of an Iron Age hill fort dating back around 2500 years. It is one of only a few Iron Age hill forts in the New Forest.

Turn right along the track, Castle Hill Lane, for 400m. After passing **Black Bush Cottages** turn left at the footpath sign through a gate and follow the path, later heading down through the trees. Cross straight over a track and keep ahead along the enclosed path, later turning right and left to run parallel with a private drive from **Burley Hill House**. Go through the small gate and keep ahead between the houses to join a road. Turn right for 30m and, at the walking sign for Burley, cross over and follow the enclosed raised path parallel to the road. Soon descend back to the road, go through a gate and cross over again, before turning left towards Burley. ▶

Keep ahead, passing the Old Farmhouse tea room, to reach a junction, with a triangular-shaped island and war memorial cross, with the Burley Inn on the right (SU 211 030); to visit the home of New Forest Cider turn right along

On the way look out for the old stone marker post opposite the entrance to Burley Manor Hotel; dated 1802, it is one of several around the village.

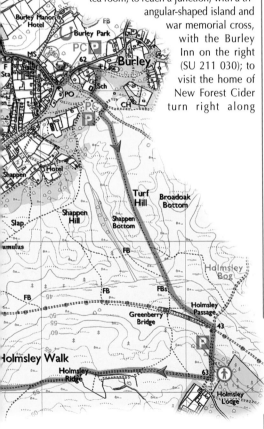

119

Pound Lane for 300m (01425 403589; www.newforestcider.co.uk).

Burley probably takes its name from the Saxon words meaning 'the fortified village in the clearing', referring to the Iron Age hill fort on Castle Hill. The first mention of the manor was in 1212 when Roger de Borlegh held the lands. The present Burley Manor, built in 1852, became a hotel in the 1930s. During the 1950s, the village was home to one Sybil Leek (1917–1982), a 'white witch' who often walked around the village with Mr Hotfoot Jackson, her pet jackdaw, perched on her shoulder. Sybil's former home near to the Queens Head now houses a shop called A Coven of Witches.

The Queens Head in Burley

From the junction turn left towards Brockenhurst, Lyndhurst and Lymington and keep left at the next junction, with the Queens Head on the left, heading along Chapel Lane. After a short distance turn right up Church Lane to reach the **Church of St John the Baptist**.

A witch and broomstick on the side of A Coven of Witches

The **Church of St John the Baptist**, which dates from 1838, has an impressive collection of vivid stained-glass windows spanning 120 years, the earliest being from the Victorian restorations in the 1880s. More recent windows include one to Constance Applebee, who died at the ripe old age of 107 in 1981 and who was responsible for introducing women's hockey into America. There is also a colourful Millennium Window and one celebrating the life of Squadron Leader Vernon Churchill Simmonds of Manor Farm, who was a Spitfire pilot during the Battle of Britain.

Turn right opposite the church, heading up the gravel track just left of the vicarage, later passing between the cricket pitch and Burley Primary School. Cross over the road and turn left, following the road for 100m, and then turn right along a gravel track into Burley car park. After 75m turn left along a broad track and, after 120m, bear half right following a well-defined track over **Turf Hill** for 1.2km (¾ mile), later descending to cross a gravel causeway over **Holmsley Bog**. The path soon splits; take the left fork through the heather to join a road just to the left of a house at **Holmsley Passage** and turn right uphill to reach the car park on the left.

WALK 18

Wilverley Inclosure and Castleman's Corkscrew

Start/finish	Wootton Bridge car park (SZ 250 997), 6.6km (4 miles) south-west of Brockenhurst
Distance	10.5km (6½ miles) or 8km (5 miles)
Time	3hrs or 2¼hrs
Maps	OS Explorer OL22
Refreshments	The Old Station Tea Rooms at Holmsley (01425 402468)

From Wootton Bridge car park the route follows a short section of the old Southampton and Dorchester Railway, known as Castleman's Corkscrew, before heading west through Wilverley Inclosure. After stopping off at the Station House at Holmsley, the route fords Avon Water, which is usually shallow and easy to cross, and meanders its way back through Brownhill Inclosure and Wootton Coppice Inclosure. Two shortcut sections are also included for anyone wanting a slightly shorter walk.

From the car park turn left, following the wide verge up the right side of the road for 250m. Shortly before the

Cyclists heading along the old railway, known as Castleman's Corkscrew

junction turn right past a vehicle barrier and along a track, following it as it bends left, and then go right along the disued railway for 700m.

> The old railway was once part of the **Southampton and Dorchester Railway**. Promoted by Charles Castleman, the line opened in 1847 following the opening of the line between London and Southampton in 1840. Primarily built to serve the market towns of Ringwood and Wimborne, the line became known as Castleman's Corkscrew due to the twisting route it followed. The opening of the present line through Bournemouth in 1888 started the gradual decline of Castleman's Corkscrew and the line closed in 1964.

About 100m after passing over a bridge turn right for 20m and then right again, heading back westwards, and shortly afterwards turn right to go under the railway bridge. Follow the grassy path north for 400m with some bushes on the right, before bending slightly left up along a shallow valley – **Yewtree Bottom** – passing to the left of a lone pine tree. Cross straight over the road and follow the access track to Wilverley Inclosure car park (SU 253 006).

Keep ahead through the gate into **Wilverley Inclosure** and follow the gravel cycle track straight on for 300m to reach the second cycle track junction; here you have to decide between a shortcut or the main route.

> **Wilverley Inclosure** was first enclosed, or fenced, in 1775 as mentioned on the small cast iron plaque close to the track. However, the trees did not grow and the inclosure was 'thrown open' to the forest, only to be re-enclosed in 1809 and planted with oaks, some of which can still be seen. It was opened again in 1846 and finally re-enclosed in 1896. Today Wilverley Inclosure is a mix of conifers and broadleaved trees.

Shortcut
Keep ahead along the gravel cycle track for 900m to rejoin the main route at a crossing ride at SU 241 010 and continue straight on; the main route comes in from the right.

For the main route turn right along the cycle track for 300m, ignoring a path off to the left on the way. Turn left along the ride through the trees and at the junction fork right (almost straight on), still following the ride northwest through the trees to a T-junction. Turn left along a wide ride and at the three-way split follow the grassy ride to the left for 600m to join a cycle track at SU 241 010. Turn right (the shortcut comes in from the left) to reach a track junction
(SU 240 011).

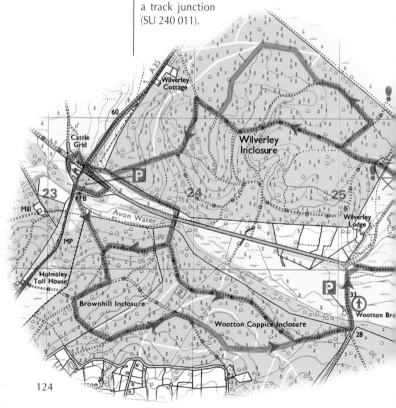

Turn sharp left and follow the cycle track downhill for 450m to reach a junction with a crossing path. Turn right, following the path down through the trees in a south-westerly direction for 500m to leave the inclosure through a large gate (SU 234 006).

The route crosses the old railway bridge and then doubles back under it, heading north

If you don't want to visit the Station House at Holmsley then turn left alongside the fence to continue the route; otherwise turn right along a path to the corner of the wood and then bear left down towards the road. Follow the enclosed path under the A35 and head northwards to soon reach a wooden electricity pole. Turn left through the trees and cross a stile to join a road at a junction. Cross over and follow the road opposite (signposted to Lyndhurst) round to the left to reach the entrance to the Station House at Holmsley on the left (SU 231 006).

125

The former railway station at Holmsley is now a great place for a cream tea

The Old Station Tea Rooms occupies the former Holmsley Station on the Southampton and Dorchester Railway. Holmsley was used as the fictional station 'Browndean' in Robert Louis Stevenson's 1899 novel *The Wrong Box*.

Suitably refreshed, retrace your route back under the A35 to reach the gate at the edge of Wilverley Inclosure (SU 234 006). Stay outside and follow the path south-east for 500m with trees to the left and turn right to follow the raised gravel path under the bridge. Here you have to ford **Avon Water**; usually this is quite shallow, but at times of high water levels care is required (see optional detour). Once across the stream go through a gate and climb gently up through the trees of **Wootton Coppice Inclosure** to join a cycle track (SU 238 001); here the shorter and longer routes diverge again.

Detour

To avoid fording Avon Water, from the Station House retrace your steps back to the T-junction and turn right under the bridge. Go right at the next junction (road for Christchurch and New Milton) and at Osmonds Bushes car park on the right, just before the A35, turn left through the bushes and over a stile. Cross the **footbridge** over Avon Water and head diagonally left across the field to a gate in the fence. Follow the path up through Brownhill Inclosure to join a gravel cycle track at SU 233 001; for the shorter route turn left, for the main route turn right.

Shortcut

For a shortcut route missing out Brownhill Inclosure, turn left at SU 238 001, following the cycle track for 1.5km (1 mile) through **Wootton Coppice Inclosure**. Go through the gate and turn left along the road, crossing over Avon Water to return to the car park.

To follow the main route, turn right along the cycle track heading for **Brownhill Inclosure**. Ignore the track to the left, but follow the cycle track as it bears round to the left (with the detour joining the main route at SU 233 001). At the T-junction turn right, then left at the next junction and immediately keep left at the split to follow the track as it bends left to finally head in a north-easterly direction. At the next track junction, with a ride ahead, turn right along the track for 100m and, where the track curves right, keep straight on along a ride through **Wootton Coppice Inclosure**, ignoring a ride on the left. Keep left at the junction and head down through the trees; ignore a ride on the left and take the left fork at the split. Turn right along the cycle track and leave the inclosure through the gate. Turn left along the road crossing over Avon Water to return to the car park.

WALK 19
Lyndhurst and Bolton's Bench

Start/finish	War Memorial at Bolton Bench car park (SU 303 081) beside the junction of Beaulieu Road (B3056) and the A35 just east of Lyndhurst town centre
Distance	10.5km (6½ miles) or 8.1km (5 miles)
Time	3hrs or 2¼hrs
Maps	OS Explorer OL22
Refreshments	Pubs, cafés, restaurants and shops at Lyndhurst

This walk takes you past Bolton's Bench and along The Ridge, with views over the open heath, then heads south through the mixed woods of Denny and Parkhill Inclosures to the east of Lyndhurst. The route then meanders its way northwards and follows Beechen Lane from where you can either head for The Ridge and retrace the outward route back past Bolton's Bench or take in a visit of bustling Lyndhurst. A slightly shorter walk missing out Parkhill Inclosure is also described.

Take a short detour up the slope for the views.

From the War Memorial head east along the surfaced track with **Bolton's Bench** up to the right. ◄

> **Bolton's Bench**, a small hillock crowned with a large yew tree, is named after the Duke of Bolton, Lord Warden of the New Forest in the 18th century. The view looking west towards Lyndhurst is dominated by the tall spire of St Michael's and All Angels Church, while to the east beyond the cricket pitch are the open heather and gorse-covered sandy heaths of White Moor.

Continue along the track, with the cricket ground and thatched pavilion on the right. At the split keep straight on along the stony track, passing a car park, with a **cemetery** over to the left. Keep ahead, soon passing to the left of a trig point and seat, following **The Ridge** with views over White Moor. To the right is the

Park Pale, which is passed on several occasions during the walk.

Bolton's Bench, a well-known landmark in Lyndhurst

> The **Park Pale** is the remains of an earth bank and ditch that once formed the boundary of a medieval deer park known as Lyndhurst Old Park, first mentioned in the late 13th century. On the top of the bank would have been paling fence to stop the deer escaping.

After a short descent, keep ahead at the junction as the track bends towards the road and fork right at the clump of silver birch (SU 322 074).

Cross over the road (B3056) and past the vehicle barrier, following a track down to the left: on the right are the remains of the Park Pale again. At the T-junction, with trees ahead, turn right for a few metres and then left down the track through trees to **Holmhill Passage**. Cross the stream and shortly go through the gate into **Little Holmhill Inclosure**, which has a varied mix of broadleaved trees. Continue for 350m, going uphill at first then levelling off, and where this track through **Denny Inclosure** bends

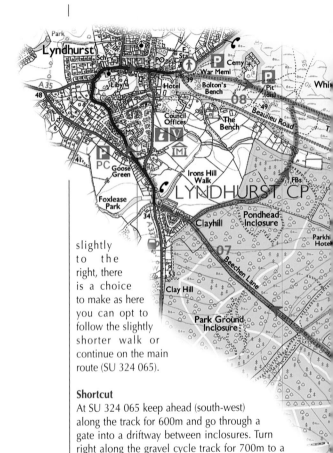

slightly to the right, there is a choice to make as here you can opt to follow the slightly shorter walk or continue on the main route (SU 324 065).

Shortcut

At SU 324 065 keep ahead (south-west) along the track for 600m and go through a gate into a driftway between inclosures. Turn right along the gravel cycle track for 700m to a track junction (SU 314 062) to rejoin the main walk.

For the main walk, turn left, heading south-east down the grassy ride to cross a small stream and then uphill, before levelling off across **Little Holm Hill**, ignoring side routes. Go through the gate and bear right across the grass and then right along a gravel cycle track. The route now follows this track for 1.2km (¾ mile) through **Parkhill Inclosure** to reach a junction of three tracks and two rides (SU 321 051).

At the junction go slightly right, ignoring the gravel cycle tracks, and go past the wooden barrier to follow the Frohawk Ride.

The **Frohawk Ride** is dedicated to the memory of the naturalist Frederick William Frohawk (1861–1946) who made many visits here in search of butterflies. Among the species that may be seen here are the silver-washed fritillary (July to August) and the pearl-bordered fritillary (May to June).

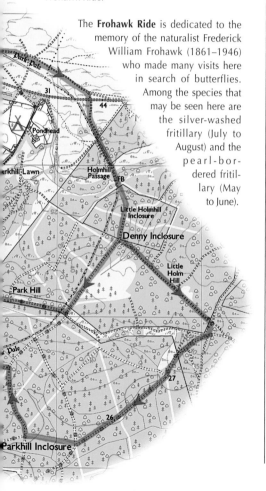

At the far end of the ride pass another wooden fence to join a gravel cycle track at a T-junction. Turn right and at the split fork left to continue along the gravel cycle track for 700m, crossing the Park Pale at SU 314 057. Go through the gate to a cross-tracks junction (SU 314 062); the shortcut rejoins here from the right. Turn left to follow the cycle track – Beechen Lane – between **Park Ground Inclosure** and **Pondhead Inclosure**, for 1.4km and go through the gate across the track (SU 303 071). Here there is another choice: either to follow the main route back to the car park, or to take in a visit of **Lyndhurst**.

For the main route, turn right through another gate and follow the track, with the trees of Pondhead Inclosure to the right. ◄

Keep left at the junction and shortly afterwards the track takes you past a small plaque on an old tree trunk on your left at William's Copse. ◄

Keep ahead along the track and through a gate, then pass between the houses and through another gate. Continue along the gravel drive and cross straight over the road (B3056). Pass the vehicle barrier, following the track up a short rise to reach the track on The Ridge that was the earlier outward route. Turn left and retrace the route past Bolton's Bench back to the start.

Alternative route

To visit **Lyndhurst**, at SU 303 071 continue straight along the road and turn right at the T-junction to follow alongside the **A337** towards the town. Keep left at the split, with the triangular-shaped green to the right. Cross straight over at the next junction, going along **Shrubbs Hill Road** to reach a T-junction beside the Queen's House. Turn right along the A35 and soon fork right up a path to the **Church of St Michael and All Angels**.

Follow the path anti-clockwise round the south side of the church, passing the plain grave of Alice Hargreaves, and continue round the church before heading down the steps to rejoin the road opposite the Crown Hotel. Turn right along the High Street (A35). ◄ At the eastern edge

The woods are a good place to see bluebells in early summer.

900 sessile oaks were planted here in 1979 to commemorate the creation of the New Forest by William I in 1079.

To visit the New Forest Centre and Museum, turn right along a lane beside the Lyndhurst Workmens Club.

LYNDHURST

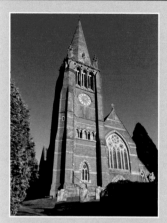

Imposing Victorian architecture – the Church of St Michael and All Angels in Lyndhurst dominates the High Street

Lyndhurst, often called the 'capital of the New Forest', was once a royal hunting lodge, first mentioned in the Domesday Book as Linhest; the name is of Saxon origin and means 'lime wood hill'. The Queen's House (or The King's House when a king is on the throne) was once the residence of the Lord Warden of the Forest. Here, too, is where the ancient Verderers Court is held to oversee the smooth running of the Forest. Step inside the imposing Victorian Church of St Michael and All Angels to see stained glass by Edward Burne-Jones and a fresco, *The Parable of the Wise and Foolish Virgins*, by Lord Leighton. In the churchyard is the grave of Mrs Hargreaves (d.1934), née Alice Liddell, who was the inspiration for Lewis Caroll's *Alice's Adventures in Wonderland* (1865); Lewis Caroll was the pen name of Charles Lutwidge Dodgson (1832–1898). The town is also home to the New Forest Centre and Museum (023 8028 3444; www.newforestcentre.org.uk).

of town, just after passing the Lyndhurst Park Hotel, turn right along the **B3056** towards Beaulieu and the car park is on the left.

The Parable of the Wise and Foolish Virgins fresco by Lord Leighton in the Church of St Michael and All Angels at Lyndhurst

WALK 20
Ashurst figure-of-eight

Start/finish	Ashurst (New Forest) Rail Station (SU 334 101); car parking at station or in Ashurst, 2.2km (1¼ miles) west on the A35 from the junction with the A326
Distance	Southern loop: 8.8km (5½ miles); Northern loop: 7.5km (4¾ miles)
Time	Southern loop: 2½hrs; Northern loop: 2hrs
Maps	OS Explorer OL22
Refreshments	The New Forest, Ashurst (023 8029 2721); shops and pubs in the village

This figure-of-eight walk from Ashurst, which has good rail links, is split into two distinct parts: the southern loop and the northern loop, allowing them to be either walked together, or as two separate walks. The southern loop heads through Churchplace and Deerleap Inclosures before crossing the railway and meandering over open heath and passing through Matley Wood on the way. A short section along the beautiful Beaulieu River makes a great place for a lunch stop before heading back to Ashurst. From here you can either finish the walk, or continue with the northern loop which goes through mixed broadleaf and conifer woods and passes the recently restored Costicles Pond, the largest example of a Mediterranean, or temporary, pond in the forest.

Southern loop

Starting from Platform 2 at Ashurst rail station head north along the enclosed path parallel to the platform, go through a gate and bear right (this track leads to the car park and village). Immediately turn right through another gate, now heading south along a narrow field parallel with the railway (right) to reach the far left corner.

> The **railway**, which now forms parts of the line from London Waterloo to Weymouth, was opened by the Southampton and Dorchester Railway in 1847. The local station was known as Lyndhurst Road until it was renamed Ashurst (New Forest) in 1997.

The route follows a broad cycle track through Churchplace Inclosure

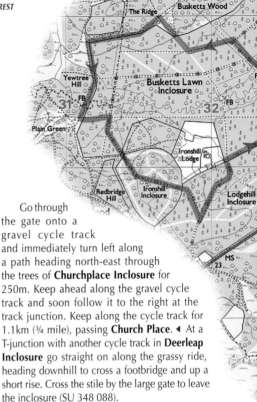

Go through the gate onto a gravel cycle track and immediately turn left along a path heading north-east through the trees of **Churchplace Inclosure** for 250m. Keep ahead along the gravel cycle track and soon follow it to the right at the track junction. Keep along the cycle track for 1.1km (¾ mile), passing **Church Place**. ◀ At a T-junction with another cycle track in **Deerleap Inclosure** go straight on along the grassy ride, heading downhill to cross a footbridge and up a short rise. Cross the stile by the large gate to leave the inclosure (SU 348 088).

This was the site of a former royal hunting lodge.

Continue ahead for 40m, passing some Scots pine, and turn right down the broad track, keeping parallel to the fence on the right for 600m. Where the cycle track turns right through a gate, keep straight on through the trees to cross the railway bridge. Follow the track across **Fulliford Bog** and fork right at the split (straight on), heading for the trees in the distance and ignoring all crossing paths. Continue up through the oak and holly trees of **Matley Wood** for 600m and shortly before the low vehicle barrier at **Matley Heath campsite**, turn right beside a large old tree trunk. Follow the indistinct path heading north down to the edge of the trees and a cross path junction (SU 331 079).

Go straight on, following the
path through the heather, and
cross a **footbridge** in the
trees. Turn left
to follow
the north

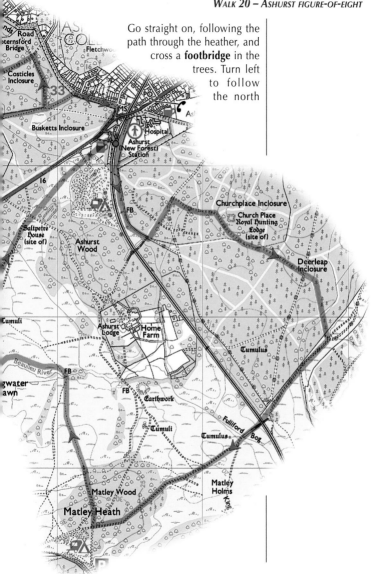

Looking east back along the Beaulieu River at Longwater Lawn – a great place for a lunch stop

This stretch alongside the river is a great place for a picnic.

bank of the **Beaulieu River** through **Longwater Lawn** to reach a footbridge – with adjacent small boundary stone (marking the boundary of the Parish of Colbury) – close to some trees. ◄

> The **Beaulieu River**, formerly known as the River Exe, flows for 19.3km (12 miles) from its source near Lyndhurst through the eastern half of the New Forest, passing Beaulieu and Buckler's Hard to join the Solent; the last 6.5km (4 miles) of the river are tidal.

Don't cross the bridge over the river; instead turn right, heading north-east away from the river, with woods over to the left and later a few oak and holly trees to the right. Keep straight on through the trees, ignoring a split to the left, to eventually reach a low vehicle barrier. Cross straight over the surfaced driveway and continue towards the building in the distance. Cross the driveway for **Ashurst campsite** and then over a footbridge. Ahead is the **New Forest pub**. Here you can either continue with the northern loop, or head for the rail station.

To finish the walk, head over to the far right corner of the field and through the gap to enter the station car park.

To continue with the walk via the northern loop, head diagonally left to a stile in the fence near the bus stop, turn right alongside the A35, passing the entrance to the New Forest pub and rail station to reach a T-junction (SU 334 103), then follow directions for the northern loop.

Northern loop

If only walking the northern loop, leave the rail station via Platform 1 and walk through the car park, passing round the New Forest pub, and turn right alongside the A35 to a junction (SU 334 103).

Either way, turn left along **Woodlands Road** for 350m. Follow the road as it curves left and use the wide grassy strip on the left. At a slight right bend, shortly after Busketts Way on the right, turn left by a wooden

The New Forest pub sign at Ashurst

pylon and go through the gate, following the path through the trees. At the T-junction turn right and then right again after 15m, heading alongside **Costicles Inclosure**, with the old boundary ditch on the left. Turn left along the gravel cycle track and at the T-junction, where the cycle track goes left, turn right and cross a **footbridge** over Bartley Water.

Keep to the gravel track as it bends left and then continue straight on along the gravel cycle track. When this turns right go straight on along the ride for a few metres and then left along another grassy ride. Turn right at the cross junction and shortly leave **Busketts Lawn Inclosure** via a small gate. Follow the fence on the left, soon turning left to continue beside the fence – the path can be indistinct in places. Ignore a gate on the left and on reaching the fence corner turn left, now heading south, with a more open area to the right. Continue following the fence and cross a couple of small streams before crossing the **footbridge** over Bartley Water (SU 311 104).

Shortly after the footbridge turn left to re-enter Busketts Lawn Inclosure, following the grass ride to a track junction. Turn right along the gravel cycle track and follow it as it bends to the left and goes slightly uphill through **Ironshill Inclosure**, passing some tall, slender oak trees. At the cycle track T-junction in Lodgehill Inclosure, turn left. ◄ Cross the gravel driveway and go straight on along the gravel cycle track. At the next junction turn right to keep along the cycle track.

Soon the red-brick Ironshill Lodge can be seen through the trees.

At the end of the long straight, ignore a ride off to the right and follow the track as it bends to the left for a few metres and then turn right along a ride, heading east for 40m to a split. Take the left fork through **Busketts Inclosure**; after 200m there is a gap in the fence on the right giving access to Costicles Pond.

> **Costicles Pond** is the largest example of a Mediterranean, or temporary, pond in the forest. These ponds are wet in winter and dry in summer, making it a harsh environment where only certain species can survive. The pond, which was used for ice skating in Edwardian times, was drained in the 1960s and has only recently been restored, bringing the pond back to life.

Keep ahead to a junction, ignore the first path on the left and at the second bear left, retracing the route back through a gate. Turn right alongside Woodlands Road and then right along the A35 before turning left back to the rail station.

WALK 21
Beaulieu Road and Bishop's Dyke

Start/finish	Beaulieu Road Station (SU 349 063), about 5.5km (3½ miles) south-west of Lyndhurst on the B3056 (car parks at Beaulieu Road and Shatterford), or Pig Bush car park (SU 362 050)
Distance	9.7km (6 miles)
Time	2½hrs
Maps	OS Explorer OL22
Refreshments	Drift Inn (023 8029 2342) and Beaulieu Hotel (023 8029 3344), both at Beaulieu Road Station

Beaulieu Road Station, home to the Beaulieu Hotel, the Drift Inn and a large number of wooden horse pens, is the starting point of this fairly level walk that crosses several boggy sections by footbridges and gravel causeways. First, the route crosses Shatterford Bottom to reach Denny Wood and then goes past sections of Bishop's Dyke to reach Pig Bush (an alternative start for car drivers). After passing an eerie pool with decaying trees, the walk heads across Yew Tree Heath and Black Down back to Beaulieu Road Station.

From the westbound platform at Beaulieu Road Station go through the car park and turn left along the road (if starting from Beaulieu Road car park head back to the road and turn right). Over to the right are a large number of wooden **horse pens**. Cross the bridge over the railway and turn left into Shatterford car park (SU 348 063).

The **horse pens** are used during the Beaulieu Road Pony Sales. Originally held in Lyndhurst, the sales were relocated to Beaulieu Road to make use of the railway to transport animals. The sales are typically held five times a year in May, August, September, October and November.

The railway, which now forms parts of the line from London Waterloo to Weymouth, was originally built by the Southampton and Dorchester Railway. The station, opened in 1847, is located about 6km

Looking back over the route from Shatterford Bottom towards Beaulieu Road Station

north-west of Beaulieu and is said to have been built as a concession to Lord Montagu, as the railway crossed his land.

Go through the car park, following a path heading south-west away from the entrance through the line of trees. Continue along a good path through the heather, crossing **Shatterford Bottom** on a gravel causeway and footbridge and keep straight on. Fork left at the split and then keep left again, keeping the trees of **Denny Wood** to the right, with open heath and a few silver birch to the left.

Denny Wood is claimed to be one of the most beautiful ancient woodlands in the forest, with magnificent mature oak and beech; the poor clay soils produce massive spreading oaks rather than tall straight ones.

Follow the path south and soon dog-leg into the trees to follow a path slightly

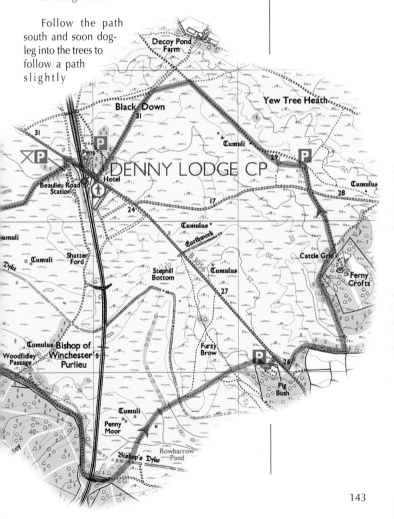

downhill and start heading south-west again through the trees, staying close to the edge of the wood. Soon bear left out of the trees to cross a footbridge and gravel causeway (SU 336 053).

Head across the open grass, aiming for another footbridge, and then along a wide grassy path to cross another footbridge. The area around here is good for spotting fallow deer, especially early or late in the day, and also for seeing hobby hawks hunting in the summer. ◄ Keep ahead with the fence of **Denny Lodge Inclosure** over to the right and at the cross tracks, with a gate over to the right, keep straight on through the open trees, still keeping parallel to the fence on the right. Follow the path as it bends to the right; the remains of **Bishop's Dyke** are on the left now with a line of older trees along the top. Keep along the track and soon a railway bridge can be seen.

A hobby looks like a large swift with long pointed wings.

> **Bishop's Dyke** is an earth bank and ditch that follows a rather convoluted route for 7.3km (4½ miles), enclosing around 500 acres of fairly boggy ground, known as the Bishop of Winchester's Purlieu. No-one really knows the purpose of the earthwork, although legend has it that John de Pontoise, Bishop of Winchester, built it around 1284 after he was given permission to enclose an area of land that he could crawl around in a day.

At SU 349 043 follow the track over the railway bridge and continue between the fences for 100m to reach a junction of paths. Fork slightly left, heading north-east through open trees, and pass a large stand of trees, crossing over Bishop's Dyke and aiming for the path visible on the horizon; to the left is **Penny Moor**. Cross a footbridge and a couple of gravel causeway sections through boggy ground and cross Bishop's Dyke again, following the stony path up the slope. At the split keep right and then left at the next; continue straight on at the cross paths, with the trees of Pig Bush over to the right. After 150m, bear right by a lone Scots pine to reach **Pig Bush car park** (SU 362 050).

A section of Bishop's Dyke near Penny Moor

Turn left along the access track and right alongside the road for 100m. Shortly before the trees, turn left across the road and take the path ahead, keeping the trees to the right. Follow the path as it bends right and continue through open trees with a fence and open field to the right for 250m. Turn left and cross three plank footbridges and a raised section through the boggy area, and then head slightly uphill along a stony path with trees over to the right. Soon the path heads through the trees and passes a small, eerie **pond** with partially submerged trees.

Keep along the path as it bends to the right to reach a gravel track leading to **Ferny Crofts**. ▸ Turn left and follow the track out to the road, then cross straight over and go along the concrete track, before turning left into **Yew Tree Heath car park** (SU 364 063).

Ferny Crofts is now home to a National Scout Activity Centre.

Several paths radiate out from the car park. Take the one heading north-west across the open heath, passing just right of the trig point; there are two parallel paths that join shortly after the trig point. Continue straight on along

145

The eerie pond with dead trees at Ferny Crofts

The tumulus is the remains of a Bronze Age bowl barrow, or burial mound, about 20m in diameter and 2.5m high.

the clear path over **Yew Tree Heath**. To the left is a gorse-covered **tumulus** (SU 358 065). ◄

At the cross paths turn diagonally left along a narrower path across **Black Down** to reach a surfaced track that leads to **Decoy Pond Farm**. Turn left alongside the track and soon pass Beaulieu Road car park in the trees to join the **B3056** with the Beaulieu Hotel, the Drift Inn and rail station opposite.

WALK 22

King's Hat, Dibden Bottom and the Beaulieu River

Start/finish	King's Hat car park (SU 386 054), west of the A326 near Hythe, or Marchwood car park (SU 392 073)
Distance	10km (6¼ miles)
Time	2¾hrs
Maps	OS Explorer OL22
Refreshments	None on the walk, several choices nearby

From King's Hat car park the walk passes through King's Hat Inclosure and alongside Crab Hat Inclosure onto Beaulieu Heath, with distant views of the Fawley Oil Refinery. Then it's along the edge of Dibden Inclosure, with views to the west over Dibden Bottom towards Yew Tree Heath (Walk 21) to reach Marchwood Inclosure (the walk may be started from the car park here). At the western end of the inclosure pass a tree-crowned tumulus and head south past Rushbush Pond before crossing the Beaulieu River. After a short walk alongside the grassy expanse of Gurnetfields Furzebrake, it's back across the Beaulieu River to the car park.

From the north side of the car park follow the grass track diagonally right along the edge of the trees, with open heath to the left, and turn left alongside the road for 125m. Turn right across the road, go through a gate and follow the track through the trees of **King's Hat Inclosure**, which dates from 1843, ignoring tracks off to the left and right. At the T-junction turn right, following the track as it curves left, and go through a large gate. Follow the track over the open heath and then alongside **Crabhat Inclosure**. Keep to the main track as it starts to climb and then levels off, with the chimneys of Fawley Oil Refinery visible in the distance. Keep to the main track at it curves left and continue for about 50m, ignoring a crossing path. Fork left at the split, still following the main stony track, now heading northwards gently down towards the trees, which are over to the left.

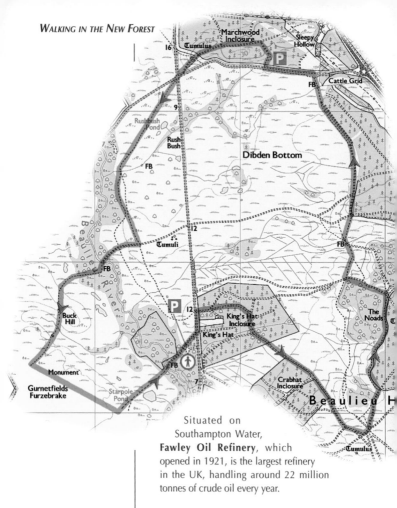

Situated on Southampton Water, **Fawley Oil Refinery**, which opened in 1921, is the largest refinery in the UK, handling around 22 million tonnes of crude oil every year.

Just after the dip (SU 399 051) turn left, following a good path with the trees of **Dibden Inclosure** to the right and views over to the left. Where the path drops to a dip, which can be boggy, follow the path just inside the wood before rejoining the main path. Continue along the path, with trees on both sides now, to reach a small open area.

Turn left following the trees on the left, with the open ground to the right, and go downhill to a path T-junction at the lower edge of the trees (SU 397 059).

Turn right along the path to reach a **footbridge** and gravel causeway. Once across, the path splits; take the right fork uphill, and ignore the crossing path to reach a flat area of gravel with views to the west over **Dibden Bottom**. Continue northwards down the short steep slope, following the wide stony path. ▶ Keep to the main path, passing a gravel causeway, and then continue gently downhill with the trees to the right. Cross the **footbridge** to join a road and turn left.

In the distance you can see Southampton.

Turn right along the access track to **Marchwood car park** and, at the far end of the car park, follow the gravel track past the metal vehicle barrier. Go left at the T-junction and follow the track heading west through **Marchwood Inclosure**, ignoring two tracks to the right. Follow the path out of the trees to reach a tree-crowned **tumulus**, or Bronze Age burial mound. ▶

This makes a great place for a sit-down or a picnic.

Gravel causeway and footbridge at Dibden Bottom

A gravel causeway and a footbridge get you across the Beaulieu River

Head down to the crossroads at Ipley Cross and continue in the same direction (between the Beaulieu and Lyndhurst roads), following a path through the heather and passing to the right of **Rushbush Pond**. On reaching the trees bear left to cross the stream and follow the path, with the trees over to the right, for 500m to reach a cross path junction. Turn right towards the trees and keep ahead to cross the gravel causeway and footbridge over the **Beaulieu River** (SU 380 060).

Keep ahead over another gravel causeway and leave the trees behind. Follow the path as it bends to the south and climbs slightly to cross **Buck Hill**. Drop down to cross a stream and continue south-west to reach **Gurnetfields Furzebrake**.

Gurnetfields Furzebrake is a large area of flat, open grass forming one of the Forest's many lawns where commoners' stock come to feed. 'Furze' is a local word for gorse.

Turn left along the left edge of the grass for 600m. ▶ Turn left down a path to pass just left of **Starpole Pond** and go ahead into the trees to cross a footbridge over the Beaulieu River. Keep ahead through the trees to reach the car park.

On the way there is a small stone memorial over to the left, marking the spot where a member of the New Forest Hounds was accidentally killed while out hunting.

New Forest ponies resting near the Beaulieu River

WALK 23
Stubby Copse Inclosure and Balmer Lawn

Start/finish	Balmer Lawn car park (SU 303 031) beside the junction of the A337 and B3055 near the Balmer Lawn Hotel; alternatively, Tilery Road car park (SU 308 032) or Brockenhurst rail station (SU 301 020)
Distance	8.2km (5 miles)
Time	2¼hrs
Maps	OS Explorer OL22
Refreshments	None on the walk; range of pubs, restaurants and shops in Brockenhurst

A fairly easy walk meandering through the mixed conifer and broadleaved woods just to the north-east of Brockenhurst and passing the site of the former Victoria Brick and Tile Works. The return leg heads through Stubby Copse Inclosure and Pignal Inclosure before crossing the flat expanse of Balmer Lawn, a favoured place for commoners' stock to graze. Just north-west of the start of this walk is Home Park, where the New Forest and Hampshire County Show has been held since 1955 (last week in July; www. newforestshow.co.uk; 01590 622400). If you are using public transport the walk may also be started from Brockenhurst rail station, although this does add 2.4km (1½ miles) to the route.

Alternative start
If starting from Brockenhurst Station, turn left (north) along the A337 for 1km, crossing over at the zebra crossing and passing Brockenhurst College. Just after crossing the Lymington River turn right for 50m along the B3055 towards Beaulieu to reach Balmer Lawn car park on the right.

From Balmer Lawn car park, standing

with your back to the Lymington River, turn right along the road (**B3055**) for 300m and fork left (straight on) along the gravel track, soon passing **Tilery Road car park** (SU 308 032). Continue along the track, with **Balmer Lawn** over to the left, and at the split fork left, slightly uphill, to reach **Standing Hat car park**. Do not go through the gate but turn right instead; go past the vehicle barrier and follow the track which forms part of the driftway between the fenced inclosures. After a short distance follow the track as it bends right through a gate into **Pignalhill Inclosure** (SU 316 035). ▶

First enclosed in 1846, Pignalhill has a mix of mature oak and beech with some conifers.

Continue along the gravel cycle track and keep left at the junction; the other track leads to **Victoria Tilery Cottage**.

Victoria Tilery Cottage was once the manager's house for the adjacent Victoria Brick and Tile Works that was built by Josiah Parkes in the 19th century. The factory, of which nothing remains today, manufactured tile-pipes that were used to drain sub-surface water from many of the forest lawns.

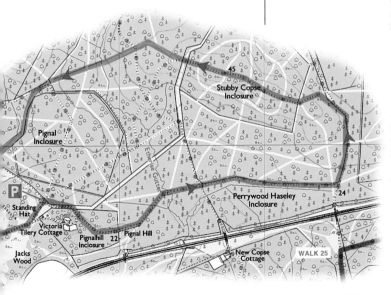

153

Follow the main gravel cycle track through the woods, ignoring any rides, and crossing **Etherise Gutter** on the way to reach a cross-tracks junction. Continue straight on, following the gravel cycle track through **Perrywood Haseley Inclosure** for slightly over 900m to reach another cross-tracks junction (SU 334 037).

Turn left, following the gravel cycle track northwards. Ignore the crossing ride, and at the next cycle track junction turn left to follow the track gently up through **Stubby Copse Inclosure** (first enclosed in 1829). ◄

There is a mix of conifers and broad-leaved trees here, including oak and beech.

Go through the gates either side of the driftway and follow the gravel cycle track for about 30m and where it bends left go straight on along the grassy ride. Ignore a ride off to the right and shortly bend left to a junction with a crossing gravel cycle track (SU 321 046).

The wide open expanse of grass at Balmer Lawn – a favoured place for commoners' stock to graze

Go straight over the gravel cycle track and follow the ride gently downhill. Cross the stream and keep ahead to a junction with a gravel cycle track. Go straight on along the cycle track for 75m and fork left down a grass ride.

Ignore the crossing ride, keeping ahead to reach a small gate in the fence. Leave the inclosure and keep ahead through the oak trees to reach the large grassy expanse of Balmer Lawn.

> **Balmer Lawn**, originally believed to have been called Palmers Lawn, is an extensive area of grassland. The low mounds are tussocks of purple moor grass that have been intensely grazed over the years. Although there are a few drainage channels, during the wet winter months the 'lawn' can become quite waterlogged.

Continue straight on in a south-westerly direction, crossing three footbridges to reach a small **pond** on your right. (If you started from Tilery Road car park turn left here heading south-east to reach the car park in the trees.)

To return to Balmer Lawn car park keep straight on and pass through some trees. Turn right with the buildings, and later **Balmer Lawn Hotel**, on your left and shortly pass to the left of the cricket pitch and clubhouse before crossing the road to arrive back at the car park.

> **The Balmer Lawn Hotel**, originally built as a hunting lodge at the start of the 19th century, was transformed into the present building some 50 years later. The hotel was commandeered during both World Wars. In the First World War it was used as a field hospital for those injured in action. Some of those that unfortunately did not survive are buried at the nearby St Nicholas' Church (see Walk 24). During WWII the hotel was used as an Army Staff College.

WALK 24
Brockenhurst and Dilton

Start/finish	Ivy Wood car park on the B3055 (SU 315 024), 1.5km (1 mile) east of Brockenhurst, or Brockenhurst Rail Station (SU 301 020) – which adds 500m to the walk
Distance	10.5km (6½ miles)
Time	2¾hrs
Maps	OS Explorer OL22
Refreshments	Pubs, cafés and shops at Brockenhurst

From Ivy Wood car park the walk follows the Lymington River through Ivy Wood towards Dilton and passes Roundhill Campsite and the remains of an ancient burial mound. The route then heads south alongside Beaulieu Heath, site of a former WWII airfield before going through Roydon Woods Nature Reserve (also visited on Walk 27) to visit St Nicholas' Church, believed to be the oldest in the Forest. If you have time, it is worth taking a short detour to explore picture-postcard Brockenhurst, before following a permissive path back to Ivy Wood. If you are travelling by public transport you can easily start from Brockenhurst Rail Station.

Alternative start

If starting from **Brockenhurst Rail Station**, exit from the east side of the station (Platform 3/4) and go through the car park south of the level crossing. Cross over the A337 and go along Mill Lane (B3055 towards Beaulieu). At the left-hand bend the main route joins from the right between Mulberry Cottage and Reynolds Cottage (SU 304 021) and goes along the road.

For the main route starting in Ivy Wood car park, stand with your back to the road and follow the path through the trees towards the **Lymington River**. Turn left, following the meandering path beside the river through **Ivy Wood** until you reach a fence; there are several small side streams to cross though most have footbridges.

The **Lymington River** rises at Ocknell Plain to the north of the A31 and joins the Solent at Lymington. Upstream from Brockenhurst the river is known as Highland Water.

The tranquil Lymington River at Ivy Wood

The path now bears left up away from the river towards the road and turns right at the fence corner to reach a grassy area and path after a short distance. Turn right, heading south, and continue along the undulating path for 900m. Shortly after crossing a small stream keep ahead along the gravel track up past some cottages at **Dilton**. Go along the concrete track over **Furze Hill** (ignoring a bridleway to the right) to reach **Roundhill Caravan Park and Campsite** (SU 332 016).

Fork right (straight on) along the surfaced track towards the old water tower visible in the trees of Stockley Inclosure to reach a track junction where the surfaced track turns to the left; over on the left is the fenced remains of the **Pudding Barrow**. ▶

Turn right, passing a low vehicle barrier, and follow the track ahead alongside the thin strip of trees for 1.5km (1 mile), with **Beaulieu Heath** over on the left.

The Pudding Barrow is a good example of an early Bronze Age (2000–1400BC) round barrow, or burial mound, one of a group on Beaulieu Heath.

157

Beaulieu Heath

was the site of the WWII Beaulieu Airfield (USAAF Station AAF-408), which became operational in 1942. The Ordnance Survey map shows the outline of the perimeter track as a large, six-sided circuit, and even though the concrete runways have been removed, they can be distinguished in places as long strips of short vegetation and are still clearly visible in aerial photographs.

Shortly after a path joins from the left, turn right to cross a bridge and then go through a large gate to follow a tree-lined track (bridleway) past **Little Dilton Farm** to a track junction (SU 329 002).

Turn right (now sharing the route with Walk 27, though in the opposite direction) and then left at the next junction. Follow the track as it bends to pass **Dilton Gardens** and enters **Roydon Woods Nature Reserve**.

Roydon Woods Nature Reserve, owned by the Hampshire and Isle of Wight Wildlife Trust, has a range of habitats from ancient woodland to wet and dry heath, along with a rich and varied wildlife. Throughout the reserve, there are five short trails to explore.

Keep ahead along the track, with **Calvesleaves Copse** to the left, later bearing right to reach a junction. Turn left down the track (bridleway – Brockenhurst 2 miles) and cross the footbridge over Lymington River; to the right is **Roydon Manor** (see Walk 27). Continue ahead along the track and after passing a large gate turn right at the T-junction, following the track to reach another junction (SU 313 005).

ST NICHOLAS' CHURCH

Believed to be the oldest church in the Forest, the Parish Church of St Nicholas has Saxon herring-bone masonry and the south doorway is a fine example of Norman work with chevron mouldings. The Purbeck stone font is also Norman. The Imperial War Graves Commission cares for the graves of 100 soldiers who were among the thousands of casualties of WWI brought over from France for treatment in the wartime Brockenhurst Hospital. The churchyard is also the resting place of Harry 'Brusher' Mills (1840–1905). To see his carved gravestone head north-west past the church into the lower graveyard and shortly on the right is the white New Zealand War Memorial – just close to the path is his grave. For many years he had the unusual job of snake catching; armed with just a forked stick and a sack it's claimed he caught over 30,000 snakes during his lifetime. His nickname 'Brusher' came about from him brushing, or sweeping, the cricket pitch before a match at Brockenhurst.

St Nicholas' Church, Brockenhurst, believed to be the oldest church in the Forest

At the junction keep right uphill (Walk 27 is the track to the left), passing to the right of a **disused pit**. Continue along the bridleway for 1.4km through the wood, on reaching the far side of the trees bear left to pass a gate, leaving Roydon Woods Nature Reserve. Keep ahead along the enclosed bridleway to join a lane opposite Beech Tree Cottage and turn right to shortly arrive at the **Parish Church of St Nicholas**.

Stand looking at the church and bear slightly right to follow the track just to the right of the church to join **Mill Lane** (B3055) between Mulberry Cottage and Reynolds Cottage on the edge of Brockenhurst (SU 304 021); if you started at the rail station or wish to visit the village, turn left here and then right along the A337. To continue with the main walk turn right along Mill Lane and, just after passing the North Lodge gatehouse, turn right through a kissing gate opposite a house.

Brockenhurst, known as Broceste in the Domesday Book, is well worth a look, whether for the picture-postcard thatched cottages, the ponies and donkeys that roam freely around the town, or the pictur-esque ford, the Watersplash, at the western end of Brookley Road. There are also cafés and shops and several pubs, including The Snakecatcher named after Harry 'Brusher' Mills. Brockenhurst is also home to the New Forest and Hampshire County Show (last week in July). The show dates back to 1921 when it was held at Bartley Cross, although New Park, just north of Brockenhurst, has been the show's home since 1955 (01590 622400; **www. newforestshow.co.uk**).

North Lodge is an ornate, French Renaissance style 19th-century gatehouse, forming the north entrance to the Brockenhurst Park Estate. The park was bought by Edward Morant in 1769, who built a fine Georgian mansion, although this was demol-ished in the 1960s. The Morant coat of arms can be seen above the archway. (Edward Morant also purchased Roydon Manor passed earlier).

Thatched cottage on Mill Lane

Follow the permissive path through two fields, keeping close to the field boundary on your left and crossing a stile and footbridge on the way (if access is removed just continue eastwards along Mill Lane). At the end of the second field go through the kissing gate and bear left to rejoin Mill Lane opposite a house (Longbow). Turn right and after crossing the Lymington River and a cattle grid turn right alongside the road and soon fork right through the trees to reach the car park.

WALK 25

Hatchet Pond and Hawkhill Inclosure

Start/finish	Hawkhill car park (SU 350 018), 2.1km (1¼ miles) west of Hatchet Gate on the B3055; alternatively, Hatchet Pond (SU 369 016) or Rans Wood car park (SU 366 024)
Distance	7.6km (4¾ miles) or 10km (6¼ miles)
Time	2hrs or 2¾hrs
Maps	OS Explorer OL22
Refreshments	During the summer there is usually an ice cream van at Hatchet Pond car park

This fairly easy walk sets out from Hawkhill car park and heads across open heath to reach Hatchet Pond – a favoured spot for picnics and fishing. Then it is off past Furzey Lodge and through Rans Wood, before passing through Hawkhill Inclosure and Frame Wood to reach Frame Heath Inclosure. Here the main walk heads south back to the car park, while the longer alternative route skirts round Ladycross Inclosure and heads along the edge of Beaulieu Heath, site of a former WWII airfield, before arriving back at the car park.

From Hawkhill car park head back along the access track for a few metres and turn left, heading east alongside the

Hatchet Pond, created in the 18th century, is now a favoured spot for a picnic

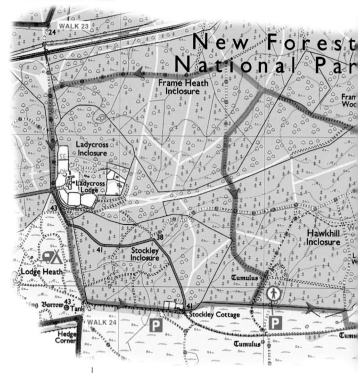

trees. At the gate on the left, bear right and then left alongside the road (**B3055**) for 250m to a slight right-hand curve in the road (about 150m before a stand of trees). Cross over and follow a narrow path through the heather just right of an ancient **earthwork** for 500m and turn left onto a gravel track just before reaching a wet, boggy area. Follow the track for 450m, soon with **Hatchet Pond** over to the right. Turn right at the junction, following the track towards the water, and then bear left following the pond.

Hatchet Pond, which was created in the late 18th century to provide waterpower for an iron mill, is now a favoured place for a picnic or a spot of coarse fishing. The pond is stocked with the likes of roach, bream, tench and carp.

At the split take the right-hand path alongside the shore as it bears left and then right through the trees. Keep following the water's edge on your right to reach the access track for Hatchet Pond car park (SU 369 016 – alternative start).

Turn left along the track and cross over the road (B3055), heading north over the heath towards **Furzey Lodge**, later joining Furzey Lane. After the last house on the left, fork left to reach Rans Wood car park. Continue past the low vehicle barrier, heading north-west down along the cycle track signposted for Brockenhurst, passing through **Rans Wood**. Keep ahead, go through a gate and follow the track up through **Hawkhill Inclosure** for 400m and, where the track bends left, continue straight on along a ride through the trees on **Moon Hill**. After 500m pass a gate and keep ahead through the oak trees of **Frame Wood**. Go through a large gate to enter **Frame Heath Inclosure** and continue slightly downhill for 125m to a junction (SU 349 033).

Here you have a choice to follow the main route or to take the longer route via Ladycross Inclosure.

To continue on the main route, turn left for 400m and then left again along the gravel cycle track, later passing through two sets of gates to reach a cycle cross-track junction. Go straight on, cross **Worts Gutter** and follow the cycle track as it later curves to the left to a cross-track junction. Turn right and soon leave the inclosure; keep ahead for 20m before turning left to reach the access track leading back to Hawkhill car park.

Alternative route

At SU 349 033 keep ahead for 300m and at the junction take the second on the left, following the cycle track west for 1.2km (¾ mile) and pass a cattle grid to reach a T-junction. Turn left along the gravel track with **Ladycross Inclosure** to the left to join a road at a corner (SU 335 026).

Go straight on alongside the road (B3055), crossing over to use the verge on the right. At the left bend fork right past the low vehicle barrier and continue straight on along the concrete track with **Roundhill Caravan Park and Campsite** over to the right; later there is the fenced-off Pudding Barrow over to the right, the remains of an early Bronze Age (2000–1400BC) round barrow, or burial mound. At the cross-track junction, next to the old WWII water tower, which was used by Beaulieu Airfield, turn left to head east along a track through the trees, keeping **Stockley Inclosure** to the left, to reach a house (Stockley Cottage) on the left.

Cross over the road (B3055) and go straight on, keeping the trees of Hawkhill Inclosure to the left and the flat, open expanse of Beaulieu Heath to the right. Cross over the cycle track and turn left at the next track back to the car park.

Beaulieu Heath was the location of the WWII Beaulieu Airfield (USAAF Station AAF-408), which was mainly used as a base for anti-submarine patrol work. The site was handed back to the Forestry Commission in 1959 and the runways were removed, although the perimeter track was left and

Beaulieu Heath

Heading towards Hawkhill Inclosure

is shown on the Ordnance Survey map; the outlines of the runways are still visible in aerial photographs. Just to the south-east, on Bagshot Moor between the B3054 and East Boldre was the site of East Boldre Airfield, which opened in 1910 when William McArdle and J Armstrong Drexel set up the New Forest Flying School.

WALK 26

Beaulieu River from Beaulieu to Buckler's Hard

Start/finish	Pay and display car park in Beaulieu (SU 386 021), off the B3056 behind Beaulieu Garage
Distance	7.7km (4¾ miles)
Time	2¼hrs
Maps	OS Explorer OL22
Refreshments	The Montague Arms Hotel and Monty's Inn at Beaulieu (01590 612324), tea rooms and shops along the High Street; The Master Builder's House hotel and Yachtsman's bar (01590 616253) and Captain's Cabin Café (01590 616203) at Buckler's Hard

This is a fairly level out-and-back walk from picturesque Beaulieu, ancestral home of Lord Montagu and site of the world-famous National Motor Museum. It also visits historic Buckler's Hard. It was here that some of Nelson's famous ships were built, each one requiring between 2500 and 3000 mature oak trees from the Forest. If there's time, visit the Maritime Museum, or during the summer take a short boat trip down the Beaulieu River. The return route follows a riverside path for part of the way, with lovely views of the river. Once back in Beaulieu you can follow a short detour to visit Beaulieu Church, or a longer diversion to visit the National Motor Museum, Lord Montagu's stately home and the remains of the Cistercian abbey.

Beaulieu, tucked alongside the Beaulieu River, was the site of a monastery founded in 1204 after King John granted his former hunting lodge known as Bellus Locus Regis ('the beautiful place of the King') to the Cistercian monks. However, most of the abbey fell into ruin after Henry VIII's Dissolution of the Monasteries. Some of the stone was used to construct castles at nearby Hurst (Walk 29) and Calshot; the remainder was sold to Sir Thomas Wriothesley, 1st Earl of Southampton. The abbey refectory became Beaulieu Church and the great gatehouse was incorporated into the present Palace House, ancestral home of the Montagu family. Most of the village forms part of the Beaulieu Estate and on many of the properties you'll see displayed the three vertically aligned red diamonds on a white background – part of the Montagu family crest.

From the car park head east along a gravel path signposted for Buckler's Hard, passing the Old Bakehouse Tea Rooms. Cross over the High Street and follow the enclosed path between the buildings, signposted 'Buckler's Hard 2 miles'. Go through the kissing gate and follow the path to the left and right to pass another kissing gate and join a gravel track; the return route arrives back here.

Turn right and go through the gate, following the enclosed gravel track, later passing a cattle grid, and continue along the gravel path. Go through some trees at **Jarvis's Copse**, crossing a footbridge, and continue through the field, following the trees on the left towards **Bailey's Hard** (SU 394 013).

Bailey's Hard was where the first naval ship, HMS *Salisbury*, was built on the river in 1698. Later it was the location of the Beaulieu Brick and Tile Works, which were built in 1790 and closed in 1935; the tall red-brick kiln chimney can be seen through the trees. The works (now a private residence) made use of local deposits of clay.

Beaulieu River at Buckler's Hard – a great place for waterfowl and boats

Go left and right past Brickyard Cottage and continue along the gravel track, going right at the junction and then left, following a track past a wooden barrier; about 100m beyond is a path off to the left, this is the return route. Follow the track through **Keeping Copse** to reach the far side of the wood; on the left through the small gate and along the wooden boardwalk is the **Keeping Marsh Bird Watching Hide**.

Follow the track to the right and in a short while cross the access road to the **Agamemnon Boat Yard**, then turn left along the signed path, with a car park on the right. At the river, turn right along the riverside path past a

171

BUCKLER'S HARD

The picturesque 18th-century hamlet of Buckler's Hard was once a bustling shipyard. The Master Builder's House, now a hotel and bar, was built in 1729 and was the home of the Master Shipbuilder. The most famous tenants were Henry Adams and his sons Balthazar and Edward, Master Builders of ships for Nelson's Navy, including three which fought at Trafalgar – *Swiftsure*, *Euryalus* and Nelson's favourite, the 64-gun *Agamemnon*. Inside St Mary's Chapel, created in the front room of one of the cottages, is a wooden plaque to Sir Francis Chichester, who set sail to circumnavigate the world in 1966–7 aboard Gipsy Moth IV. To find out more about Buckler's Hard, visit the Maritime Museum (www.bucklershard.co.uk; 01590 616203), or between Easter and October take a 30-minute boat trip along the river.

Cottages at Buckler's Hard on the Beaulieu River – three ships that fought at the Battle of Trafalgar were built here

Known as the Duke's Bath Cottage, this cottage was built in 1760 by the Duke of Montagu at a time when saltwater was considered beneficial for arthritis.

small, picturesque thatched cottage, to reach **Buckler's Hard** on the banks of the Beaulieu River (SU 409 001). ◄

Take time to explore: follow the gravel track northwards between the two rows of cottages passing the Master Builders House Hotel and St Mary's Chapel; shortly off to the left is a track to the **Maritime Museum**. Retrace your steps back to the river and turn left along the riverside path. Cross over the boatyard road and shortly after the gate leading to the Keeping Marsh bird

Statue of the Virgin Mary at the Buckler's Hard chapel

hide, fork right along the path signed 'Riverside Walk to Beaulieu'.

> The **Riverside Walk**, which crosses several foot-bridges and goes along boardwalks, offers views across the Beaulieu River and takes you through part of the North Solent National Nature Reserve. The reserve, which is well known for its populations of overwintering and migratory waterfowl, has a range of habitats, from ancient woodland to mud-flats and salt marsh.

After 1.2km (¾ mile) the path bears left to rejoin the gravel track (SU 396 012); turn right, right again at the first junction and then left to pass Brickyard Cottage again.

Mill pond and Palace House at Beaulieu – viewed from the B3056 beside Beaulieu Garage

Keep ahead, retracing the outward route back towards Beaulieu to reach the kissing gate (SU 388 021). Do not turn left through the gate, but instead continue along the gravel track which takes you past the old and new fire station to reach the main road, with the **Montagu Arms Hotel** on your left. To complete the walk, turn left along the road past the hotel and then left at Monty's, following the High Street. After a short distance turn right across the road and follow the gravel path back to the car park.

To visit Beaulieu Church

The mill pond was created in medieval times by monks from the abbey to provide water power for the corn mill.

At the Montague Arms Hotel turn right along the **B3054**, soon crossing the river, with the tidal mill pond on the left. ◀ Follow the road round to the right then slightly left and turn left across the road and follow the driveway past the cattle grid to reach the **church**; retrace the route back to the hotel and follow the directions in the main route to return to the car park.

To visit the National Motor Museum

A visit to the National Motor Museum (01590 612345; www.beaulieu.co.uk) will add 2.4km (1½ miles) to the walk. Turn left at the hotel, following the main road, cross over at Beaulieu Garage, and soon fork right along the signed path beside the **B3056**; to return retrace the outward route back to the village.

WALK 27
Setley Common and Boldre Church

Start/finish	Setley Pond car park (SZ 302 992), 3.3km (2 miles) south of Brockenhurst off the A337, or Boldre Church (SZ 324 993)
Distance	10.5km (6½ miles) or 5.3km (3¼ miles)
Time	3hrs or 1½hrs
Maps	OS Explorer OL22
Refreshments	Red Lion, Boldre (01590 673177); Hobler Inn (01590 623944) near Setley Pond; Filly Inn, Setley (01590 623449)

From Setley Pond the walk heads north and crosses the A337 at the Filly Inn and then meanders through the important wildlife haven of Roydon Woods Nature Reserve (also visited on Walk 24), crossing the Lymington River with glimpses of Roydon Manor. The route then heads south, passing the historic church at Boldre with its beautiful engraved window before visiting the village and heading back to Setley Pond. There is a shortcut if you don't want to visit the Red Lion at Boldre and a shorter walk is also described, although this misses out the visit to Boldre Church.

From Setley Pond car park head back to the road and go left for 20m and then right to follow the right-hand path northwards over **Setley Common**. ▶ Later the path

Take a look south-west towards Sway to catch a glimpse of the 66m-high, late 19th-century Sway Tower, or Peterson's Tower, still the world's tallest non-reinforced concrete building.

Setley Pond

Inside is adorned with everything from old traps to swords and horse brasses. Folklore has it that the ghost of a highwayman roams the inn at night.

bears right and runs parallel to the **A337**. On reaching the minor road, turn right over the **cattle grid** and carefully cross over the A337 to reach a lane opposite; to the left is the **Filly Inn**. ◄

Go along the lane and fork right to cross a cattle grid and pass **Setley Farm**. Continue along the track for 1.1km (¾ mile), entering **Roydon Woods Nature Reserve**, to reach a track junction next to a disused pit on the left (this section is shared with Walk 24.)

Turn right down the track for 300m to a junction (SU 315 002); here the short and long walks diverge.

Shortcut

Continue straight on and fork right at the signpost, following a bridleway up through **Fluder's Clump** and crossing a footbridge. Go through a gate to reach a four-way junction (SZ 313 997); continue straight on along the main route.

To continue the main route, turn left through the large gate and keep ahead along the enclosed bridleway, later crossing a footbridge over the **Lymington River** (SU 317 003); over to the left can be seen **Roydon Manor**. ▸

The Lymington River rises at Ocknell Plain to the north of the A31 and joins the Solent at Lymington; upstream from Brockenhurst the river is known as Highland Water.

Roydon Manor is an elegant, brick-built 17th-century building purchased by Edward Morant in 1771 (two years earlier he had bought Brockenhurst House – see Walk 24). Roydon Manor is still the Morant family home. However, the manor dates back to at least 1250 when Henry III granted it to Netley Abbey, which held it until the Dissolution of the monasteries.

Continue up the track for 400m and turn right at the junction, now following the fence on your left. Keep to the track as it bends to the left, later going right then left around **Dilton Gardens** (house) to reach a track junction. Turn right and at the next junction keep straight on (Walk 24 comes in from the left), following the track ahead for 800m towards **Haywards Farm**. Just before the house,

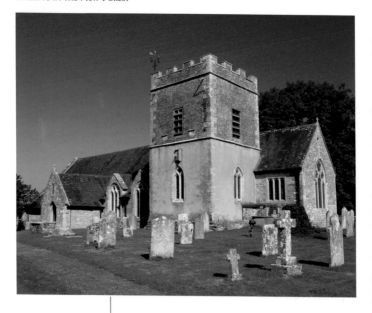

Parish Church of St John the Baptist at Boldre

turn right along the gravel drive and continue ahead along the enclosed waymarked path. Later the route passes a car park to reach a lane, with the **Parish Church of St John the Baptist** over to the right (SZ 324 993).

Sitting on a small hillock about 1.2km (¾ mile) from the village of Boldre, the **Parish Church of St John the Baptist**, dates back to the late 11th century, although there have been numerous alterations over the intervening centuries. Inside is a memorial to HMS *Hood*, a battle cruiser sunk by the German battleship *Bismarck* in 1941. Only three out of 1418 men survived. Among those who died was Vice Admiral L E Holland CB, who had been a regular worshipper at Boldre; a service is held here every May in memory of the ship's company. There is also a beautifully engraved Millennium Window by Tracey Sheppard.

Turn left (south-east) along Church Lane for 250m to a track junction on the left, here turn right down a narrow enclosed track (footpath sign) for 500m. After passing a garden nursery turn left down the lane for 120m.

To miss out Boldre village and pub visit
At the house on the left turn right along the track towards the **water works**, and just before the gate turn left and

Detail from the beautifully engraved Millennium Window at the Parish Church of St John the Baptist, Boldre

follow the perimeter fence. Bear left to cross a **foot-bridge**, go through a gate and head diagonally right across the field to a large gate. Keep ahead following the field boundary on your right to a stile and continue through the next field, keeping the scrub on your left, to reach a stile. Go up through the trees and turn right along the lane, keeping right at the junction to a crossroads at SZ 318 993 (this reduces the walk by 800m).

To continue to Boldre, keep along the lane and turn right at the junction heading towards Boldre, crossing the Lymington River to reach the **Red Lion**. Turn right along Royden Lane, signposted for Sandy Down, and later keep right at the road junction to reach a crossroads (SZ 318 993). (The shortcut missing out Boldre rejoins here.)

Go straight on for 170m and, immediately after the second house on the left, turn left at the large gate following a signed bridleway through the trees with a fence on your left. After passing a kissing gate keep ahead along the enclosed track to a junction (SZ 313 997); the shorter walk joins from the right here. Turn left over the open ground between houses, following the path signposted for the Hobler Inn. Go through kissing gates either side of the lane and follow the hedge-lined path, later descending through trees.

Cross over Lower Sandy Down Lane and take the path ahead next to the wooden electricity pole. Cross the footbridge and stile and keep ahead through the field to another stile, continue up through the next field, keeping close to the boundary on your left. Cross a stile and follow the sunken path with the trees on the right, later going left to follow the enclosed path to reach a road. Turn left past the **Hobler Inn** and once level with the car park carefully cross the A337 and follow an enclosed path just to the right of the white-painted house opposite for 300m. Cross the stile and follow the trees on the left, fork right at the house and cross over the main gravel track, following the one signed for horses and soon passing just left of Setley Pond back to the **car park**.

WALK 28

Exploring the coastline from
Lymington to Keyhaven

Start/finish	Lymington rail station (SZ 327 958); there are several car parks in town
Distance	15.7km (9¾ miles), 12.2km (7½ miles) or 8.8km (5½ miles)
Time	4hrs, 3½ hrs or 2¼hrs
Maps	OS Explorer OL22
Refreshments	Range of pubs, cafés and shops at Lymington; The Chequers Inn, Woodside (01590 673415) – short detour; Gun Inn, Keyhaven (01590 642391)

From the rail station in bustling Lymington, which is served by a branch line from Brockenhurst, the walk follows a slightly inland route, heading south-west towards Keyhaven before turning round to follow the coastal path, which forms parts of the Solent Way all the way back to Lymington. The coastal section of the walk offers great views of Hurst Castle and the Isle of Wight, and there should also be ample opportunities to see the varied range of birdlife that visits the two nature reserves. From the Middle Ages this stretch of coastline was an important centre for producing salt from seawater, until cheaper, mined salt forced the closure of the last saltern in the 1860s. The complete walk is fairly long, although there are a couple of shortcuts described, one turning back at Moses Dock and the other at Pennington Marshes; a quick look at the map will reveal other possible shortcuts.

Lymington, or Lentune as it was called in the Domesday Book, is now a thriving yachting centre; however, for several centuries Lymington flourished on the export of salt from the salt pans that stretched along the coast towards Hurst Spit. Along the High Street, home to a bustling Saturday market and some fine Victorian and Georgian architecture, is the Parish Church of St Thomas and All Saints, which dates back several hundred years, with its 18th-century cupola-crowned tower. To learn more about the town and the Solent coastline call in at the St Barbe Museum and Art Gallery, which also houses the visitor information centre (01590 676969; **www.stbarbe-museum.org.uk**).

From the **station** turn left along Mill Lane and continue to the end, dogleg right and left along a path before turning right up cobbled Quay Hill. Continue straight on up the High Street; part way along is New Street on the right, leading to the St Barbe Museum and Art Gallery. On reaching the **Parish Church of St Thomas and All Saints** turn left down Church Street for 500m. Fork left along Waterford Road and cross straight over Stanley Road. Continue along King's Saltern Road. Where the road bends left, fork right at the entrance for Lymington Yacht Haven and turn right along a signed footpath through the reeds. Turn left along winding **Normandy Lane** for 1km and at the junction (SZ 326 940) go left to follow a lane past **Eight Acre Pond**.

Continue straight on past **The Salterns**, then past a cottage, and keep along the hedge-lined path. Ignore a path to the left to pass between a couple of old brick buildings on the left and some cottages on the right at **Moses Dock**. Just past the cottages turn left over

a V-stile; here you can opt for a shortcut or continue with the main walk.

> **Moses Dock** was one of several narrow inlets built to allow barges to dock and offload coal for the boiling houses and to export the salt. The old brick buildings on the north side of the inlet are the last two remaining salt boiling houses. Seawater was held in ponds, or salterns, and left to partially evaporate, before the strong brine was pumped by windmill into large boiling pans where it was heated to form salt crystals.

Shortcut
Turn left with **Moses Dock** on the left, soon bending left to reach the sluice gate. Turn left and rejoin the main walk at SZ 327 934.

The main walk turns right to shortly join a lane. ▶ Turn left along the meandering lane, passing Oxey Barn, to its end at Oxey Farmhouse. Continue straight on along

Following the sea wall path (also the Solent Way) near Eight Acre Pond, with the Isle of Wight in the distance

The 16th-century Chequers Inn is 250m to the right.

183

Boat at Moses Dock. The dock was one of several narrow inlets built to allow barges to dock to offload coal for the boiling houses and to export the salt

the enclosed gravel path and turn left along Lower Pennington Lane as it bends to the right to reach a small parking area at SZ 318 927.

Here you can either start heading back via another shortcut or continue with the main route on towards Keyhaven.

Shortcut
Turn left through a gate, keep left at the split and turn left along the sea wall following the **Solent Way** to rejoin the main walk at SZ 325 923.

To continue to Keyhaven, go straight on past the gate and follow the enclosed gravel track. Pass another gate and continue along the lane to reach a small parking area and gate on the left (SZ 308 916).

To visit the pub
For a pub visit, continue along the lane with the small harbour

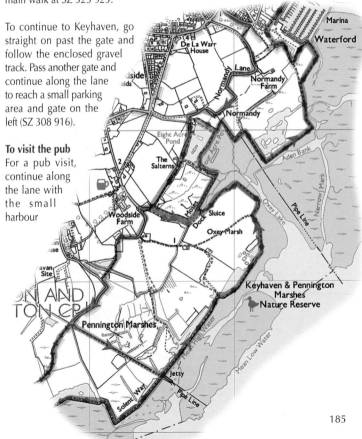

The 97km (60-mile) Solent Way connects Milford on Sea to Emsworth Harbour, passing a mix of landscapes from seafronts, yachting harbours and coastal marshland to open heath and woodland.

on the left to a T-junction, with the **Gun Inn** ahead; retrace the route back to the gate.

Turn left through the gate (or right if returning from the Gun Inn). The route now follows the Solent Way along the sea wall back towards Lymington, with great views across the two nature reserves; after 2.5km (1½ miles) the second shortcut joins from the left at SZ 325 923. ◄

The **Lymington and Keyhaven Nature Reserve** (to the landward side of the path) stretches from the mouth of the Lymington River to Keyhaven and consists of both grazing marsh and brackish lagoons, which provides feeding and roosting areas for waterfowl and supports a number of specialist plant and animal species. The adjacent coastal mudflats and salt marshes, protected by the long shingle spit that leads to Hurst Castle, form the Hampshire and Isle of Wight Wildlife Trust's **Keyhaven and Pennington Marshes Reserve**.

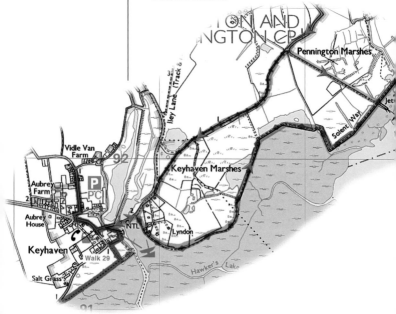

The reserves form an important stop-off point for migrating birds in spring and autumn and are major breeding sites for common terns, sandwich terns and little terns.

Continue along the sea wall for a further 2km (1¼ miles), with Pennington Lagoon and then Oxey Lagoon to the left. Follow the path as it bends left to start heading south-west and reach the **sluice gate** at Moses Dock (SZ 327 934). ▶ Turn right (left if following the shortcut) and go through the gates either side of the sluice gate before turning right, still following the sea wall. The path bends left to a path junction; here turn right to stay along the sea, with Eight Acre Pond over to the left. Ignore two paths off to the left either side of Maiden Dock and continue, following the Solent Way along the sea wall path round **Normandy Marsh**.

The first shortcut rejoins the main route here.

At the path junction (SZ 334 943) keep right along the sea wall, bending left towards the yacht marina; to the right you'll probably catch sight of the Wightlink Ferry. ▶ Do not go into the car park but turn left (Solent Way) and soon go right along a raised pathway which shortly leads through the boatyard – follow the white concrete bollards. Go right and then left along the surfaced road; to the right is the Haven Bar and Bistro. Continue straight on along the raised gravel path, with boats to the right, and soon turn left as you pass the seawater baths. ▶

Ferries started sailing between Lymington and the Isle of Wight in 1830.

Dating from 1833, this is the oldest lido in Britain (open daily in the summer).

Continue alongside the sea wall, cross the slipway and go between the car park and the Royal Lymington Yacht Club. Head diagonally left across the recreation ground and then right along Bath Road. At the junction keep ahead along Quay Street, passing the harbour (from where boats offer short trips exploring the western Solent) and small car park before continuing along the cobbled street. Where this turns left up Quay Hill, go straight on, retracing the route back along Mill Lane to the rail station.

WALK 29
Milford on Sea and Hurst Castle

Start/finish	Car park in Keyhaven (SZ 305 914; pay and display in summer), 1.7km (1 mile) east of Milford on Sea, or Milford on Sea (SZ 291 917; pay and display)
Distance	6.1km (3¾ miles) or 10.5km (6½ miles)
Time	1½hrs or 2¾hrs
Maps	OS Explorer OL22
Refreshments	Gun Inn, Keyhaven (01590 642391); Smugglers Inn, Milford on Sea (01590 644414); along with several other options not on the route

A fairly easy walk exploring the most southerly part of the New Forest. From the seaside village of Keyhaven the route takes an inland route, meandering across open fields to Milford on Sea, with its interesting Norman church. The return leg follows part of the Solent Way along the coast, with great views of the Isle of Wight and The Needles. The extended route includes a walk along the impressive 2km (1¼-mile) curving shingle spit to visit Hurst Castle. From here you can either walk back to Keyhaven, or jump on the seasonal passenger ferry, which saves about 3.3km (2 miles) of walking.

Turn right out of the car park to pass the **Gun Inn**. Ignore the side road and at the next junction go right along Lymore Lane, following it as it quickly turns to the left. Shortly after the last house, where the lane curves left, turn right over a stile beside a large gate and follow the surfaced track between open fields. At the end, turn left and then right over a stile, following a path alongside of the fence on the left to reach a stile in the far left field corner opposite a thatched cottage. Turn left along **Agarton Lane** and when it bends to the right, fork left at the footpath sign, just after the trig point. Follow the path southwest across the field to the far side (SZ 296 926).

Go right along **Lymore Lane** for 50m and at the footpath sign turn left, following a path across the middle of the field to a junction of four paths and a wooden finger post.

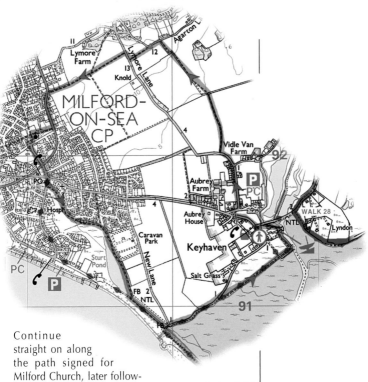

Continue straight on along the path signed for Milford Church, later following a garden boundary on the right to reach the field corner. Go through to Lymington Road (**B3054**) and turn left for 250m. Just before the junction with Church Hill, turn right across the road and through a small metal gate following a path into the churchyard. At the split take the left fork, passing just left of **All Saints Church**. Leave through the lychgate and go right along Church Hill, following it as it soon bends left to a reach a crossroads at SZ 291 919.

Although **All Saints Church** has seen many alterations, much of it dates from the 12th and 13th centuries. Inside there are memorials to the Cornwallis-West family, local landowners in the 19th century, and in the north-west window of the chancel is a stained glass panel showing Charles I, who was imprisoned in nearby Hurst Castle. Outside the church, just to the right of the entrance, are two 14th-century grotesque heads above the window: one a man playing bagpipes and the other a woman with a medieval hairstyle.

Just to the left is the Smugglers Inn.

Go straight over through **Milford on Sea**, keeping the village green on your right, to another crossroads. ◄

Milford on Sea, first mentioned as Melleford in the Domesday Book, has a long history stretching back to Saxon times. Between 1107 and 1539, the village belonged to Christchurch Priory, and for several centuries Milford remained a small village with a scattering of thatched cottages. In the 1880s, Colonel Cornwallis-West (1835–1917) of Newlands Manor tried to change the village into a 'fashionable' seaside resort similar to what his friend, the Duke of Devonshire, was doing at Eastbourne; luckily for the historic village the venture failed.

The Solent Way is a 97km (60-mile) long-distance coastal walk from Milford on Sea to Emsworth Harbour.

Go straight over at the crossroads, heading along Sea Road and, just after crossing the stream, turn left into the car park, keeping close to the stream and left side of the car park. At the far left corner continue straight on along a gravel path, signposted 'Solent Way'. ◄

Keep ahead as the path runs beside some houses for a short distance, with reed beds on the right. Ignore paths off to the left and soon the gravel path passes along the edge of **Sturt Pond**. Go right over the **footbridge** and up the shingle bank. From here there are impressive views to the south-east along the shingle spit towards Hurst Castle and lighthouse, to the south across the Solent to the Isle of Wight and The Needles and west across Christchurch Bay to Bournemouth and the Purbeck Hills. Turn left and follow the top of **Hurst Spit** for 300m to reach a large boulder and plaque (SZ 299 908). ◄

Hurst Spit is a shifting shingle barrier beach, protecting the western approach to the Solent and sheltering large areas of salt marsh and mud flats.

Here there is a choice of either heading directly back to Keyhaven or extending the walk to visit Hurst Castle.

To walk back to Keyhaven turn left at the top of the shingle, following the path down across the footbridge over the stream from Sturt Pond. Continue along Saltgrass Lane heading north-east for 350m, with the sea on the right. On a high spring tide (nothing to do with the season, but rather the time of the new moon or the full moon when the sun, moon and earth are approximately aligned) this road is liable to flood; however, there is a higher path just to the left of the road if needed. Just after passing the flood gate, fork right through a kissing gate at the Solent Way sign and follow the gravel path beside the sea wall.

After 450m, either turn left along a gravel path back to Keyhaven, or continue alongside the sea wall, soon turning left to pass the small jetty from where the ferry to and from Hurst Castle operates. Continue alongside the sea wall, cross over the surfaced track beside the yacht club, and follow the Solent way signs, with the harbour

Heading along the shingle of Hurst Spit towards Hurst Castle and lighthouse

HURST CASTLE

Situated at the end of the long shingle spit, less than a mile (1.3km) from the Isle of Wight, Hurst Castle was built by Henry VIII in 1544 to defend the western approach to the Solent. The castle is one of a series built to defend the coastline. Just over a century later Charles I was imprisoned here in 1648 before being taken to London for trial and execution. The building was extended during the Napoleonic Wars and again in the 1870s, when the large armoured wings with 38-ton guns were constructed. The castle remained part of Britain's coastal defences until 1956. The original lighthouse was built in the 1780s to help guide vessels through the hazardous western approaches to the Solent between The Needles and the shingle bank; the current lighthouse was built in 1867 (castle information, including the ferry: 01590 642344; www.hurstcastle.co.uk).

The lighthouse on Hurst Spit, built in 1867

on your right. Turn left along the lane to reach the car park on the left.

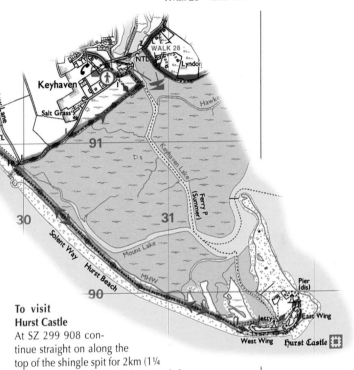

To visit Hurst Castle

At SZ 299 908 continue straight on along the top of the shingle spit for 2km (1¼ miles) to reach Hurst Castle. Bear left at the split, following the signs for the castle entrance (SZ 317 897); the path continues to reach the lighthouse (SZ 318 899). From the castle you can either retrace your outward route back along the shingle spit or, in summer, you can take the easy option and jump on the small ferry (daily service April–October, limited winter weekend service, weather permitting) that operates from the **jetty** beside the castle to Keyhaven harbour, from where it's a short walk back to the car park.

Alternatively, to walk back to Keyhaven retrace the outward route back to the boulder and plaque at SZ 299 908 and from the top of the shingle spit turn right to rejoin the main route back to the start.

WALK 30
Lepe and Exbury

Start/finish	Lepe Country Park (SZ 455 985; Lower Beach pay and display car park), or Lepe Western car park (SZ 452 985; pay and display)
Distance	9.7km (6 miles) or 7.3km (4½ miles)
Time	2½hrs or 2hrs
Maps	OS Explorer OL22
Refreshments	Lepe Country Park shop and café (023 8089 2991)

From Lepe Country Park, a busy place during WWII, the route follows a coastal path with views across the Solent to the Isle of Wight. Part of the path follows the foreshore, which sometimes floods at high tide – just follow the parallel road instead. At the mouth of the Beaulieu River the route heads inland to Exbury, where a short detour leads to the famous Exbury Gardens. The return section meanders across open fields back to the country park. A shorter route missing out Exbury is also described.

The area around **Lepe** (once a favoured haunt of smugglers until the Coast Guard Cottages and Watch House were built in the 19th century) played an important role in the D-Day landings, both as a major departure point and for the construction of some of the Mulberry Harbours. It was also the mainland base for PLUTO (Pipe-Line-Under-The-Ocean), a 3-inch welded steel pipeline built to provide a ready supply of fuel for the advancing army; the pipe crossed the Solent and Isle of Wight and then went under the channel to France.

The estuary is a great place for seeing birdlife, such as little egret, common tern, shelduck and reed warbler.

From the car park at Lepe Country Park follow the coast road west, keeping the sea on your left, and cross the bridge over **Dark Water**. ◄

At the entrance to Lepe Western car park fork left and continue along the gravel footpath, keeping the sea to the left and passing the white-painted **Watch House**; above

194

The 19th-century Coast Guard Cottages

are the slate-hung Coast Guard Cottages. Keep ahead to reach the white-painted lighthouse. Here the route follows the foreshore path for 1.6km (1 mile). Occasionally the path gets flooded at high tide; if this is the case, just follow the road which runs parallel with the coast instead and rejoin the route at SZ 433 986.

> The **lighthouse** (or Beaulieu River Millennium Beacon) was built to help seafarers navigate the approach to the Beaulieu River from the Solent, which is a relatively narrow channel between Beaulieu Spit and the Lepe Foreshore.

Keep along the path, sometimes at the base of low cliffs, weaving past fallen trees or passing oak trees growing close to the water's edge. After 900m the route passes **Inchmery House**. ▶

Off the coast is the low-lying Gull Island bird sanctuary with the Isle of Wight beyond.

> **Inchmery House**, which dates from around 1780, was bought by Lionel de Rothschild in 1912, who planned to surround it with exotic gardens. Unfortunately the plan failed and in 1919 he purchased the nearby Exbury Estate instead, now the home of the Exbury Gardens.

195

The lighthouse (or Beaulieu River Millennium Beacon) built to help seafarers navigate in the Solent – the route follows the shoreline path

On reaching the road (SZ 433 986) turn left for 400m and, at the left bend, turn right over the grass and through a kissing gate by the footpath sign. Follow the enclosed path, shortly bearing right through woodland and crossing a footbridge. Continue up through the trees to cross another footbridge and reach an open field. Follow the hedge on your left round to the left and then right to pass through the hedge ahead. Ignore the path off to the right but keep straight on, with the oak wood on your left, to pass another hedge and reach a path junction and three-way path signpost at the field boundary; here you have a choice to make between the continuing the main walk or taking the shortcut.

Shortcut

Turn right following the field boundary on the left and continue past **Cump Copse**. Cross over the road and follow the bridleway, rejoining the main route at SU 439 000.

To continue the main walk, turn left along a path just inside the wood. Soon follow the path right and then bear left. Leave the trees and continue over the field to cross a stile in the hedge and turn right along Inchmery Lane for 600m to **Exbury** (SU 426 001).

The village of **Exbury** was originally located at Lower Exbury near the mouth of the Beaulieu River and it was here that the first chapel was built. In the early 19th century William Mitford, Lord of the Manor of Exbury and Lepe, decided to build a new village at Upper Exbury, which now forms the present village. The old chapel was demolished and a new church was built, incorporating materials from the old church, including the bell dated 1509. The present church is dedicated to St Katherine of Alexandria, patron saint of medieval wheelwrights; she was martyred on a spiked wheel, in about AD300.

Detour to gardens and church

To visit either the **Parish Church of St Katherine** or Exbury Gardens keep ahead at the junction towards Beaulieu for 100m to the church or a further 300m for the gardens; retrace the route back to the junction.

> The world-famous **Exbury Gardens**, with their colourful collections of rhododendrons, azaleas, camellias and rare trees, were developed by Lionel de Rothschild after he bought the Exbury Estate in 1919. Meandering through part of the garden is a 12-inch narrow-gauge steam railway. There is also a restaurant and tea room (023 8089 1203; **www. exbury.co.uk**).

To continue the main walk, turn right (or left if coming back from the church or gardens) along the road towards Lepe and Blackfield for 150m and then go left along the lane signposted for The Crescent, passing a large tree and some old petrol pumps. Near the end of the lane turn right at the footpath sign along the enclosed track. After passing through a gap in the hedge follow the track left and then right to enter **Horsemoor Copse**. ◄

This is a good place to see bluebells in early summer.

Continue through the trees for 600m, cross a stile and turn right up the lane. At the right bend, go left over the stile next to the large gate and footpath sign. Continue along the track for 150m and, where it bends to the left, turn right along a path, following the field boundary on your left and later passing **Burnthays Copse**. Join a gravel track after 400m; the shorter route rejoins here (SU 439 000).

Bear left (right if following the shortcut) along the tree-lined track (bridleway) towards **East Hill Farm**. Where the track bends right to the farm keep left at the bridleway sign (straight on), following the enclosed bridleway, which bears round to the right. At the signed junction go right along the woodland footpath for 100m and then left to cross a footbridge and go up through the trees. Continue across the middle of the field, passing an old stile on the way. Go through the gap in the hedge next to the wooden electricity pole and continue across the field, passing just right of the trees at **Grassy Copse**.

Go through the kissing gate and keep ahead through the next field to a large gate. Follow the track, crossing a bridge, and, where the track bends to the right, go left up towards the top left field corner. Go through two small gates a couple of metres apart and follow the permissive path diagonally right across the field passing just left of the pine trees and houses to reach a kissing gate in the hedge. Turn left down through the car park, cross the road and turn left back to the start.

A short detour leads to the Parish Church of St Katherine at Exbury

APPENDIX A
Route summary table

Walk	Title	Distance	Start	Time
1	Langley Wood and Hamptworth	8.5km (5¼ miles) and 8.9km (5½ miles)	Lay-by beside River Blackwater (SU 219 203)	2½hrs or 2¾hrs
2	Godshill and Castle Hill	7.6km (4¾ miles) or 11.6km (7¼ miles)	Godshill Wood car park (SU 177 160)	2¼hrs or 3½hrs
3	Hatchet Green and Woodgreen	9.3km (5¾ miles)	Deadman Hill car park (SU 192 165)	2¾hrs
4	Bramshaw Telegraph and Eyeworth Pond	10.5km (6½ miles) or 8km (5 miles)	Telegraph Hill car park (SU 228 166)	3hrs or 2¼hrs
5	Bramshaw Church and Nomansland	8.2km (5 miles)	Pipers Wait car park (SU 249 165)	2¼hrs
6	Abbots Well and Alderhill Inclosure	8.5km (5¼ miles)	Abbots Well car park (SU 177 128)	2¼hrs
7	Fritham and Cadman's Pool	10.5km (6½ miles) or 8.5km (5¼ miles)	Fritham car park (SU 230 140)	3hrs or 2½hrs
8	Janesmoor Pond and the Rufus Stone	8.8km (5½ miles); plus 3.1km (2 miles) with extension	Janesmoor Pond car park (SU 247 136)	2½hrs (plus 1hr with extension)
9	High Corner Inn and Ogden's Purlieu	5.2km (3¼ miles) or 9.2km (5¾ miles)	Broomy Walk car park (SU 197 099)	1½hrs or 2½hrs
10	Appleslade Bottom to Rockford via Ibsley Common	9.7km (6 miles)	Appleslade car park (SU 184 092)	2¾hrs
11	Castle Piece and Linford Brook	7.7km (4¾ miles)	Linford Bottom car park (SU 180 071)	2¼hrs
12	Exploring Bolderwood	5.6km (3½ miles) or 9.2km (5¾ miles)	Bolderwood car park (SU 243 086)	1½hrs or 2½hrs
13	Minstead and Furzey Gardens	8.7km (5½ miles) or 12.5km (7¾ miles)	Acres Down car park (SU 267 097)	2½hrs or 3½hrs
14	Portuguese Fireplace and the Knightwood Oak	9.7km (6 miles)	Millyford Bridge car park (SU 267 078)	2¾hrs

Walk	Title	Distance	Start	Time
15	Bank and Gritnam	7.6km (4¾ miles)	Parking area on Pickney Lane (SU 288 067)	2¼hrs
16	Ober Water and Blackwater Arboretum	11.7km (7¼ miles) or 6.8km (4¼ miles)	Whitefield Moor car park (SU 273 026)	3¼hrs or 2hrs
17	Holmsley Walk and Burley	9.7km (6 miles)	Holmsley car park (SU 221 011)	2¾hrs
18	Wilverley Inclosure and Castleman's Corkscrew	10.5km (6½ miles) or 8km (5 miles)	Wotton Bridge car park (SZ 250 997)	3hrs or 2¼hrs
19	Lyndhurst and Bolton's Bench	10.5km (6½ miles) or 8.1km (5 miles)	Bolton Bench car park (SU 303 081)	3hrs or 2¼hrs
20	Ashurst figure-of-eight	Southern loop: 8.8km (5½ miles); Northern loop: 7.5km (4¾ miles)	Ashurst rail station (SU 334 101)	Southern loop: 2½hrs; Northern loop: 2hrs
21	Beaulieu Road and Bishop's Dyke	9.7km (6 miles)	Beaulieu Road Station (SU 349 063)	2½hrs
22	King's Hat, Dibden Bottom and Beaulieu River	10km (6¼ miles)	King's Hat car park (SU 386 054)	2¾hrs
23	Stubby Copse Inclosure and Balmer Lawn	8.2km (5 miles)	Balmer Lawn car park (SU 303 031)	2¼hrs
24	Brockenhurst and Dilton	10.5km (6½ miles)	Ivy Wood car park (SU 315 024)	2¾hrs
25	Hatchet Pond and Hawkhill Inclosure	7.6km (4¾ miles) or 10km (6¼ miles)	Hawkhill car park (SU 350 018)	2hrs or 2¾hrs
26	Beaulieu River from Beaulieu to Buckler's Hard	7.7km (4¾ miles)	Beaulieu village car park (SU 386 021)	2¼hrs
27	Setley Common and Boldre Church	10.5km (6½ miles) or 5.3km (3¼ miles)	Setley Pond car park (SZ 302 992)	3hrs or 1½hrs
28	Exploring the coastline from Lymington to Keyhaven	15.7km (9¾ miles) or 12.2km (7½ miles) or 8.8km (5½ miles)	Lymington rail station (SZ 327 958)	4hrs, 3½hrs or 2¼hrs
29	Milford on Sea and Hurst Castle	6.1km (3¾ miles) or 10.5km (6½ miles)	Keyhaven car park (SZ 305 914)	1½hrs or 2¾hrs
30	Lepe and Exbury	9.7km (6 miles) or 7.3km (4½ miles)	Lepe Country Park (SZ 455 985)	2½hrs or 2hrs

APPENDIX B
Useful contact information

Information offices
Fordingbridge Information Office
Salisbury Street, Fordingbridge, SP6 1AB
01425 654560; www.visitfordingbridge.co.uk
Lymington Visitor Information
St Barbe Museum, New Street, Lymington SO41 9BH
01590 676969; www.lymington.org
Lyndhurst Visitor Information Centre
Main Car Park, Lyndhurst SO43 7NY
023 8028 2269; www.thenewforest.co.uk
New Forest National Park Authority
Lymington Town Hall, Avenue Road, Lymington SO41 9ZG
01590 646600; www.newforestnpa.gov.uk
The Verderers of the New Forest
The Queen's House, High Street, Lyndhurst SO43 7NH
023 8028 2052; www.verderers.org.uk
Forestry Commission
The Queen's House, High Street, Lyndhurst SO43 7NH
023 8028 3141; www.forestry.gov.uk/newforest

Local information points
These local information points offer a range of maps, leaflets and publications.
Beaulieu
New Forest Activities, The Old Forge, High Street, Beaulieu SO42 7YD; 01590 612377
Brockenhurst
Melt, 17 Lyndhurst Road, Brockenhurst, SO42 7RL; 07968 786560
Burley
Burley Post Office, The Cross, Burley, BH24 4AA; 01425 402258
Hythe
Herald Publishing, 6 High Street, Hythe SO45 6AH; 023 8084 5700
Landford
Landford Village Stores, Lyndhurst Road, Landford SP5 2AJ; 01794 390242
Milford on Sea
The Village News, 74 High Street, Milford on Sea, SO41 0QD; 01590 645595
Minstead
Minstead Village Shop, The Green, Minstead SO43 7FY; 023 8081 3134
Sway
Sway Deli and Coffee Shop, 3 Middle Road, Sway, SO41 6DB; 01590 683392
Woodgreen
Woodgreen Community Shop, Hale Road, Woodgreen, SP6 2AJ; 01725 512467

Public transport information
For rail service enquiries, call National Rail Enquiries on 03457 48 49 50; www.nationalrail.co.uk

For all public transport enquiries (including buses and trains), call the Traveline on 0871 200 22 33; www.traveline.info

Bus companies
The following bus companies currently operate in the New Forest:

Bluestar Buses
01202 338421; www.bluestarbus.co.uk
Route 6: Southampton to Lymington via Ashurst, Lyndhurst and Brockenhurst
Route 8/9: Southampton to Calshot via Dibden Purlieu and Hythe

More Bus
01202 338420; www.morebus.co.uk
Route 112: Hythe; Beaulieu; Boldre; Lymington
Route 119: New Milton; Pennington; Lymington
Route X1/2: Bournemouth to Lymington via New Milton

New Forest Tour Bus
www.thenewforesttour.info
Red Route: Lyndhurst; Burley; Ringwood; Fordingbridge; Sandy Balls; Ashurst; Lyndhurst
Green Route: Lyndhurst; Brockenhurst; Lymington; Beaulieu; Exbury Gardens; Lyndhurst
Blue Route: Lymington; Brockenhurst; Burley; New Milton; Barton-on-Sea; Milford-on-Sea; Keyhaven; Lymington

Local wildlife trusts
Hampshire and Isle of Wight Wildlife Trust
01489 774400; www.hiwwt.org.uk

Animal rescue (injured animals or birds)
For sick, injured or distressed commoners' stock (pony, cow, donkey, pig and sheep):
The Verderers of the New Forest: 023 8028 2052

For other injured animals or birds, contact:
Forestry Commission: 023 8028 3141
RSPCA: 0300 1234 999

Rights of way
Hampshire County Council Rights of Way Office
0300 555 1391; www.hants.gov.uk/row

Wiltshire County Council Rights of Way Office
01225 756178; www.wiltshire.gov.uk/communityandliving/rightsofway.htm

Ramblers Association
020 7339 8500; www.ramblers.org.uk

APPENDIX C
Glossary

Agister	official employed by the Verderers, responsible for the welfare of commoners' animals
Balls	in the north-west of the Forest hills are often called 'balls'
Bottom	meaning a valley in place names
Commoner	a person using the common rights that are attached to a property where they live
Depastured	stock animals living on the open Forest
Down	area of open heathland
Drift	autumn round-up of ponies in the Forest
Driftway	unfenced routes for animals to move along between open parts of the Forest
Estovers	common right entitlement to collect wood for fuel
Fern	local name for bracken
Furze	local name for gorse
Gate	an entrance to Crown land
Gutter	meaning a stream in place names
Hat	small copse, though some are now inside large inclosures
Holm	wood of holly trees
Inclosure	area of woodland that is (or was) fenced, where stock cannot enter, originally for commercial timber production
Lawn	grassy area giving the best grazing and kept that way by continued grazing
Marl	common right to dig marl (mix of clay and lime) from the open Forest; no longer exercised
Mast	common right to release pigs to feed in open Forest during the 'pannage' season, allowing pigs to eat acorns which are poisonous to cattle and ponies
Pannage	period of year when mast can be practised; the start date is determined by the Verderers (typically when acorns fall) and it lasts for a minimum of 60 days
Passage	a causeway through a bog
Perambulation	the traditional boundary of the Forest within which Forest Law applied
Pollarded	tree cut when young to form multiple main branches (no good for ship timber)
Purlieu	part of the Forest that was freed from Forest Law
Ride	wide track through woodland
Shade	established spot where ponies and cattle regularly gather, not necessarily in the shade though
Slade	broad valley
Turbary	common right to cut heathland turf (peat) for fuel; no longer exercised
Verderers	10 officials whose main function is to protect the rights of the commoners

APPENDIX D
Bibliography

Christy, Geraldine *The New Forest: Its Character and Heritage* (Red Post Books, 2005)

Conway, Mathew *The New Forest* (The History Press Ltd, 2010)

McKay, Ian (editor) *A New Forest Reader: A Companion Guide to the New Forest, its History and Landscape* (Hatchet Green Publishing, 2011)

Ponting, Gerald *New Forest Foxglove Visitor Guide* (Foxglove Media, 2013)

Tubbs, Colin R *The New Forest: History, Ecology and Conservation* (New Forest Ninth Century Trust, 2001)

Snook, Alan Michael *Birds of the New Forest: A Visitor's Guide* (Centurion Books, 1998)

Sterry, Paul *Regional Wildlife: New Forest* (Dial House, 1995)

CICERONE GUIDES TO THE BRITISH ISLES

SCOTLAND

Backpacker's Britain: Northern Scotland
Ben Nevis and Glen Coe
Great Mountain Days in Scotland
Not the West Highland Way
Scotland
Scotland's Best Small Mountains
Scotland's Mountain Ridges
Scrambles in Lochaber
The Ayrshire and Arran Coastal Paths
The Border Country
The Borders Abbeys Way
The Cape Wrath Trail
The Great Glen Way
The Great Glen Way Map Booklet
The Hebridean Way
The Hebrides
The Isle of Mull
The Isle of Skye
The Skye Trail
The Southern Upland Way
The Speyside Way
The Speyside Way Map Booklet
The West Highland Way
Walking Highland Perthshire
Walking in Scotland's Far North
Walking in the Angus Glens
Walking in the Cairngorms
Walking in the Ochils, Campsie Fells and Lomond Hills
Walking in the Pentland Hills
Walking in the Southern Uplands
Walking in Torridon
Walking Loch Lomond and the Trossachs
Walking on Arran
Walking on Harris and Lewis
Walking on Rum and the Small Isles
Walking on the Orkney and Shetland Isles
Walking on Uist and Barra
Walking the Corbetts Vol 1 South of the Great Glen
Walking the Corbetts Vol 2 North of the Great Glen
Walking the Munros Vol 1 – Southern, Central and Western Highlands
Walking the Munros Vol 2 – Northern Highlands and the Cairngorms
West Highland Way Map Booklet
Winter Climbs Ben Nevis and Glen Coe
Winter Climbs in the Cairngorms

NORTHERN ENGLAND TRAILS

Hadrian's Wall Path
Hadrian's Wall Path Map Booklet
Pennine Way Map Booklet
The Coast to Coast Map Booklet
The Coast to Coast Walk
The Dales Way
The Dales Way Map Booklet
The Pennine Way

LAKE DISTRICT

Great Mountain Days in the Lake District
Lake District Winter Climbs
Lake District: High Level and Fell Walks
Lake District: Low Level and Lake Walks
Outdoor Adventures with Children – Lake District
Scrambles in the Lake District – North
Scrambles in the Lake District – South
Short Walks in Lakeland Book 1: South Lakeland
Short Walks in Lakeland Book 2: North Lakeland
Short Walks in Lakeland Book 3: West Lakeland
The Cumbria Way
Tour of the Lake District
Trail and Fell Running in the Lake District

NORTH WEST ENGLAND AND THE ISLE OF MAN

Isle of Man Coastal Path
The Lancashire Cycleway
The Lune Valley and Howgills
The Ribble Way
Walking in Cumbria's Eden Valley
Walking in Lancashire
Walking in the Forest of Bowland and Pendle
Walking on the Isle of Man
Walking on the West Pennine Moors
Walks in Ribble Country
Walks in Silverdale and Arnside

NORTH EAST ENGLAND, YORKSHIRE DALES AND PENNINES

Great Mountain Days in the Pennines
South Pennine Walks
St Oswald's Way and St Cuthbert's Way
The Cleveland Way and the Yorkshire Wolds Way
The Cleveland Way Map Booklet
The North York Moors
The Reivers Way
The Teesdale Way
Trail and Fell Running in the Yorkshire Dales
Walking in County Durham
Walking in Northumberland
Walking in the North Pennines
Walking in the Yorkshire Dales: North and East
Walking in the Yorkshire Dales: South and West
Walks in Dales Country
Walks in the Yorkshire Dales

WALES AND WELSH BORDERS

Glyndwr's Way
Great Mountain Days in Snowdonia
Hillwalking in Shropshire
Hillwalking in Wales – Vol 1
Hillwalking in Wales – Vol 2
Mountain Walking in Snowdonia
Offa's Dyke Map Booklet
Offa's Dyke Path
Ridges of Snowdonia
Scrambles in Snowdonia
The Ascent of Snowdon
The Ceredigion and Snowdonia Coast Paths
The Pembrokeshire Coast Path
Pembrokeshire Coast Path Map Booklet
The Severn Way
The Snowdonia Way
The Wales Coast Path
The Wye Valley Walk
Walking in Carmarthenshire
Walking in Pembrokeshire
Walking in the Forest of Dean
Walking in the South Wales Valleys
Walking in the Wye Valley
Walking on the Brecon Beacons
Walking on the Gower

DERBYSHIRE, PEAK DISTRICT AND MIDLANDS

Dark Peak Walks
Scrambles in the Dark Peak
Walking in Derbyshire
White Peak Walks: The Northern Dales
White Peak Walks: The Southern Dales

SOUTHERN ENGLAND

North Downs Way Map Booklet
South West Coast Path Map Booklet – Vol 1: Minehead to St Ives
South West Coast Path Map Booklet – Vol 2: St Ives to Plymouth
South West Coast Path Map Booklet – Vol 3: Plymouth to Poole
Suffolk Coast and Heath Walks
The Cotswold Way
The Cotswold Way Map Booklet
The Great Stones Way
The Kennet and Avon Canal
The Lea Valley Walk
The North Downs Way
The Peddars Way and Norfolk Coast path
The Pilgrims' Way
The Ridgeway Map Booklet
The Ridgeway National Trail
The South Downs Way
The South Downs Way Map Booklet
The South West Coast Path
The Thames Path
The Thames Path Map Booklet
The Two Moors Way
Two Moors Way Map Booklet
Walking Hampshire's Test Way
Walking in Cornwall
Walking in Essex
Walking in Kent
Walking in London
Walking in Norfolk
Walking in Sussex
Walking in the Chilterns
Walking in the Cotswolds
Walking in the Isles of Scilly
Walking in the New Forest
Walking in the North Wessex Downs
Walking in the Thames Valley
Walking on Dartmoor
Walking on Guernsey
Walking on Jersey
Walking on the Isle of Wight
Walking the Jurassic Coast
Walks in the South Downs National Park

For full information on all our guides, books and eBooks, visit our website: **www.cicerone.co.uk**

Walking – Trekking – Mountaineering – Climbing – Cycling

Over 40 years, Cicerone have built up an outstanding collection of over 300 guides, inspiring all sorts of amazing adventures.

Every guide comes from extensive exploration and research by our expert authors, all with a passion for their subjects. They are frequently praised, endorsed and used by clubs, instructors and outdoor organisations.

All our titles can now be bought as **e-books**, **ePubs** and **Kindle** files and we also have an online magazine – **Cicerone Extra** – with features to help cyclists, climbers, walkers and trekkers choose their next adventure, at home or abroad.

Our website shows any **new information** we've had in since a book was published. Please do let us know if you find anything has changed, so that we can publish the latest details. On our **website** you'll also find great ideas and lots of detailed information about what's inside every guide and you can buy **individual routes** from many of them online.

It's easy to keep in touch with what's going on at Cicerone by getting our monthly **free e-newsletter**, which is full of offers, competitions, up-to-date information and topical articles. You can subscribe on our home page and also follow us on **Facebook** and **Twitter** or dip into our **blog**.

Cicerone – the very best guides for exploring the world.

CICERONE

Juniper House, Murley Moss, Oxenholme Road, Kendal, Cumbria LA9 7RL
Tel: 015395 62069 info@cicerone.co.uk
www.cicerone.co.uk